Current Perspectives:
Readings from InfoTrac® College Edition

Ethics in Criminal Justice

MICHAEL WHALEN

WADSWORTH
CENGAGE Learning™

Australia • Brazil • Japan • Korea • Mexico • Singapore • Spain •
United Kingdom • United States

WADSWORTH
CENGAGE Learning™

ISBN-13: 978-0-495-59777-3
ISBN-10: 0-495-59777-5

Wadsworth
10 Davis Drive
Belmont, CA 94002-3098
USA

Cengage Learning is a leading provider of customized learning solutions with office locations around the globe, including Singapore, the United Kingdom, Australia, Mexico, Brazil, and Japan. Locate your local office at:
international.cengage.com/region

Cengage Learning products are represented in Canada by Nelson Education, Ltd.

For your course and learning solutions, visit **academic.cengage.com**

Purchase any of our products at your local college store or at our preferred online store **www.ichapters.com**

Printed in Canada
1 2 3 4 5 6 7 12 11 10 09 08

Table of Contents

Preface

Society has a profound interest in demanding ethical behavior by its police, courts, and justice professionals. These men and women have been entrusted with the responsibility of maintaining an orderly community and have been given powerful tools with which to do so. When the stewards of justice are corrupt, the impact can be devastating.

Our Criminal Justice system encompasses law enforcement, prosecutors, defense attorneys, courts, and corrections. Also involved are researchers, treatment providers, counselors, lawmakers, and government agencies. Each of these players impacts society's efforts to maintain order and punish offenders. Each of these players also must face ethical challenges in the performance of his or her duties. Whether seeking monetary gain, abusing power, or simply going too far in the pursuit of justice, members of the Criminal Justice profession face numerous opportunities to violate the rules that govern their conduct.

Defining the limits that establish "ethical behavior" on the part of government and the criminal justice system has perhaps never been more important. The "War on Terror" has presented challenges never faced before, including asking such questions as "what rights do suspected foreign terrorists have," and "how far should the government be permitted to go in the pursuit of terrorists?"

Legal ethics are often difficult to define. Is it "ethical" for a lawyer to try to win the freedom of a violent offender he knows to be guilty? The American Trial Lawyers Association's Code of Ethics is included in these pages to help answer that question. Is it "ethical" for the state to confine someone based on what he *might* do in the future? The case of Kansas versus Hendricks determined that it is indeed legal. But is it ethical? The answer may differ from person to person.

This reader encompasses the full breadth of the Criminal Justice system, from the individual police officer to the Federal government. In these pages, students will encounter a prosecutor whose thirst for a conviction was so strong that he concealed evidence that proved the defendants innocent. Also included are accounts of corruption, perjury, and misuse of power. Students will find that contemplating and understanding these issues is a crucial step in preparing for an ethical career in Criminal Justice.

Chapter 1

Law Enforcement

Practice and Policy

1

Man Arrested on Charges of Using Internet to Solicit Sex from Teen

W-B Man Believed He Was Meeting Girl, 14, but She Was a Police Decoy, Officials Say

Edward Lewis

A Wilkes-Barre man was arrested early Wednesday morning on charges he used the Internet to solicit sex from a teenage girl, who actually was a police decoy. Matthew R. Dale, 20, of Crescent Avenue, was apprehended at about 12:05 a.m. when he arrived at the White Haven Shopping Center where he expected to meet the girl to have sex in his car, White Haven police said. Dale was charged with criminal attempt to commit statutory sexual assault, criminal use of a communication facility, unlawful contact with a minor and criminal attempt to commit corruption of minors. He was arraigned before District Judge Paul Hadzick and jailed at the Luzerne County Correctional Facility for lack of $2,500 bail. According to the criminal complaint filed by officers Adam Aton and Tom Szoke, and Luzerne County Detective Charles J. Balogh: Police were posing as a fictitious 14-year-old girl named Lauren on the Internet on Tuesday and received an instant message from a person at 10:34 p.m. The person used a sexually explicit user name and identified himself as a 20-year-old male who was aware he was chatting with someone six years younger than him. A general conversation took place for several minutes before the person, identified in the criminal complaint as Dale, said he wanted to play "doctor and nurse" with the girl and described several sexual positions. Dale told the girl that he wanted to have sex in his car and agreed to meet her in front of a drug store and liquor store at the shopping center.

Police set up surveillance at the shopping center and observed a Ford Taurus enter the parking lot just after midnight. Dale turned off the car's headlights and parked. The fictitious girl called Dale and told him to pick her up in the middle of the shopping center. When Dale drove through the parking lot, police apprehended him.

Police said they found two condoms in Dale's pants pocket, the criminal complaint says. Dale admitted to police that he knew he was meeting a 14-year-old girl for sex. He told police, "I made a stupid mistake tonight," the criminal complaint says. A preliminary hearing is scheduled for March 27 in Central Court.

2

Civil Rights and Civil Liberties

Vehicle searches

Christopher Dunn

Recent disclosures about the New York City Police Department's stopping, questioning, and frisking of New Yorkers raise significant issues about the constitutionality of the department's practices.

While earlier controversies focused on race-based stops that implicated constitutional equal-protection guarantees, the information released earlier this month invites a more traditional Fourth Amendment analysis of stop-and-frisk practices because the NYPD reports indicate that a majority of stops were based on a factor the U.S. Supreme Court has ruled cannot alone be the basis for a valid police stop.

The Recent Disclosures

After the February 1999 shooting death of Amadou Diallo and the public controversy that ensued over the 41 shots fired at Mr. Diallo by four members of the NYPD's Street Crime Unit, the New York City Council passed a law requiring the department to produce, among other things, quarterly reports documenting its stopping, questioning, and frisking of New Yorkers. As of January 2007, however, the most recent data the department had produced was for the third quarter of 2003, a lag of more than three years.

In the face of an imminent New York Times story about its reporting lag, the department on Feb. 2 delivered to the City Council stop-and-frisk reports providing information about various aspects of NYPD stops during 2006. As has been widely reported, those reports disclose a dramatic increase in the number of police stops and further reveal that black New Yorkers continue to be stopped in numbers well out of proportion to their representation in the general population. Specifically, in 2006 police officers completed forms documenting 508,540 stops, as compared to having completed forms documenting approximately 97,000 stops in 2002 (the most recent, prior full year for which the department has released data). Of those whose stops were documented, approximately 55 percent were black; 11 percent white, and 30 percent Hispanic; in the general population, according to recent census data, blacks constitute approximately 25 percent, whites 35 percent, and Hispanics 27 percent.

The release of the 2006 stop-and-frisk data has sparked renewed debate about the role of race in police stops. Seeking to counter critics who have pointed to the disparities between the proportion of blacks stopped and of blacks in the general population as evidence of racial profiling, the NYPD has contended that the racial profile of those stopped is explained by the fact that over 65 percent of those identified as criminal suspects are black. This, the department has argued, explains why over half of those stopped in 2006 were black, despite blacks comprising only one quarter of the City's population.

The department's position highlights an important point about the NYPD's stop-and-frisk reports: they provide detailed information about the factors identified by the NYPD for its stops. And, setting aside for now what those factors may reveal about the role of race in police stops, the NYPD's self-reported factors raise significant Fourth Amendment questions about the department's stops.

The NYPD's reports identify 28 different factors behind stops in 2006. Among the factors are such things as "report by victim/witness/officer," "inappropriate attire for season," "proximity to scene of offense," "unusually nervous," "evasive response to questioning," "change direction at sight of officer," "suspicious bulge," and "area has high crime incidence."

The factor "area has high crime incidence" is the single most common factor listed in the NYPD reports. It is identified as playing a role in approximately 270,000 stops, constituting about 53 percent of all stops, and is the only factor identified in a majority of stops. Because the Supreme Court has specifically addressed the extent to which presence in a high-crime area can be a basis for a police stop, the newly released data open the door to Fourth Amendment analysis of the department's stop-and-frisk practices.

The Law of High-Crime Investigatory Stops

About 90 percent of the stops reported by the NYPD in 2006 did not result in formal arrest or issuance of a summons, meaning that probable cause did not exist for most of the stops. That, however, does not establish that the stops violate the Fourth Amendment for the simple reason that the Supreme Court nearly 40 years ago endorsed investigatory stops based on less than probable cause. Nonetheless, the Court repeatedly has held that the Fourth Amendment still places specific constraints on these stops and has specifically addressed the extent to which presence in a high-crime area may be a basis for a lawful police stop.

The Supreme Court's seminal ruling about police stops with less than probable cause is its 1968 ruling in Terry v. Ohio.1 That case involved three men who a veteran police officer observed "casing" a store in preparation for what the officer believed might be a robbery. After the officer stopped the men and patted down their coats, he discovered two guns and arrested the men. The Court reviewed their conviction, holding that the stop-and-frisk did not violate the Fourth Amendment. In doing so, the Court held that even an investigatory stop of a civilian triggers the Fourth Amendment but also held that such stops do not require probable cause. Rather, the Court explained, a stop is permissible if the "officer observes unusual conduct which leads him reasonably to conclude in light of his experience that criminal activity may be afoot."

The Court's decision in Terry did not present any issue about the role a person's presence in a high-crime area might play in an investigatory stop, but that express issue arose 11 years later when the Court decided Brown v. Texas. 2 That case started with the arrest of one Zackary Brown in El Paso, Texas, after two police officers observed him and another man in an alley known as a location for drug dealing. The arresting officer testified that he had stopped Mr. Brown because the situation "looked suspicious and we had never seen that subject in that area before."

When stopped, Mr. Brown refused to identify himself, which led to his arrest for violating a Texas statute requiring persons lawfully stopped by an officer to identify themselves. Mr. Brown was convicted in county court of violating the identification statute, ending up with a direct appeal to the Supreme Court. In reversing Mr. Brown's conviction, a unanimous Court focused on whether the officers had lawfully stopped him so as to trigger the statutory identification obligation.

In analyzing the stop's lawfulness, the Court started with the proposition, emanating from Terry, that the Fourth Amendment applies "to all seizures of the person, including seizures that involve only a brief detention short of traditional arrest." Such seizures, while subject to a balancing test, still must satisfy a core requirement: "the Fourth Amendment requires that a seizure must be based on specific, objective facts indicating that society's legitimate interests require the seizure of the particular individual." In those instances in which probable cause does not exist, police officers nonetheless can justify investigatory stops under this balancing test so long as the officers have "reasonable suspicion, based on objective facts, that the individual is involved in criminal activity."

Turning to the specific facts presented by Mr. Brown's stop, the Court applied these rules as follows:

Officer Venegas testified...that the situation in the alley looked "suspicious," but he was unable to point to any facts supporting that conclusion. There is no indication in the record that it was unusual for people to be in the alley. The fact that [Mr. Brown] was in a neighborhood frequented by drug users, standing alone, is not a basis for concluding that [Mr. Brown] himself was engaged in criminal conduct. In short, the appellant's activity was no different from the activity of other pedestrians in that neighborhood.

The Court therefore reversed.

Brown therefore establishes that presence in a high-crime area, "standing alone," cannot be the basis for an investigatory stop. Consistent with the "standing alone" qualification, however, the Court more recently has held that presence in a high-crime area may be a basis for a valid stop in conjunction with other permissible considerations.

In Illinois v. Wardlow, 3 a 2000 ruling that is the Court's most recent discussion of the role of high-crime presence in the Terry analysis, the Court addressed a challenge to the stop of a person who had fled from a high-crime area upon seeing officers approach. In upholding the stop the Court cited Brown for the proposition that "[a]n individual's presence in an area suspected of criminal activity, standing alone, is not enough to support a reasonable, particularized suspicion that the person is committing a crime."

Nonetheless, the Court explained that "officers are not required to ignore the relevant characteristics of a location" in determining whether to make a Terry stop and therefore stated that presence in a high-crime area might be taken into account with other factors in determining whether an investigatory stop is appropriate. And in upholding the particular stop in dispute, the Court stated, "[I]t was not merely respondent's presence in an area of heavy narcotic trafficking that aroused the officers' suspicion, but his unprovoked flight upon noticing the police."

Taken together, Brown and Wardlow provide the basic framework for considering whether police stops based on presence in a high-crime area comport with Terry. To the extent stops are based solely on that factor, they would violate the Fourth Amendment. To the extent, however, this was but one factor leading to a stop, the stop might be permissible depending upon the other factors involved.

NYPD Stops and Frisks

As noted, the NYPD's recently released stop-and-frisk reports list "area has high crime incidence" as the most common factor in last year's police stops, with it being the only factor reported as being present in a majority of the half-million stops. In light of the Supreme Court's ruling in Brown, this suggests that there may be a significant Fourth Amendment issue for many of the NYPD stops last year.

Nonetheless, the NYPD data made publicly available to date do not allow one to draw final conclusions about the propriety of department stops based on this factor. This is because the NYPD reports reveal that many stops may have been made for more than one reason. It is not possible to tell from those reports, however, how many of the high-crime stops also had other factors and, for those that did, what those specific other factors were.

To the extent other factors were part of certain high-crime stops, that then would require consideration of whether those factors, in conjunction with presence in a high-crime area, were sufficient to satisfy the Fourth Amendment standards for investigatory stops emanating from Terry. In some instances the combination of factors may be sufficient; in others it may not.

What can be said at this point is that the NYPD stop-and-frisk reports raise important questions about the constitutionality of police stops in New York City. Given the large number of reported high-crime stops and the possibility therefore that significant numbers of stops may not comport with the Fourth Amendment, it is essential to answer those questions through further review and analysis of the stop-and-frisk data underlying the recently released reports.

Christopher Dunn is the associate legal director of the New York Civil Liberties Union.

3

Breaking the Blue Wall

Chicago's Police

The Windy City's police department has an ugly history. In its most infamous chapter, officers tortured suspects in the 1970s and 1980s. But even with such a past, this year has been particularly fraught for America's second-biggest police force. The police superintendent, Philip Cline, stepped down in April after two videos emerged of off-duty officers beating civilians. Seven members of an elite unit, the Special Operations Section (SOS), face an array of charges including kidnapping, burglary and false arrest, and one officer was accused in September of plotting to kill a defector.

As a whole, Chicago's police are well behaved and effective. The number of murders in the city in 2006 was 44% down on 1995. But the scandals have officials scrambling to restore public trust. On October 9th Dana Starks, the interim police superintendent, announced that he would disband the SOS. On October 15th the Office of Professional Standards (OPS), which investigates police misconduct, issued its first quarterly report. Other recent changes include separating the OPS from the police department. But there is still much work to be done.

Craig Futterman, a law professor at the University of Chicago, wants the OPS to overhaul the way it investigates complaints. Between 2002 and 2004 civilians filed more than 10,000 reports of serious abuse, such as excessive force and false arrests. Only 19 of these complaints led to an officer's suspension for a week or more, he says. Ilana Rosenzweig, the new head of the OPS, is trying to recruit investigators, but her office is understaffed and is dealing with almost 1,300 open cases.

A broader problem is how to change the police department's culture. It is common for police officers to shield each other from punishment, but the phenomenon reaches an extreme in Chicago. Complaints of brutality were 94% less likely to be sustained in Chicago than in other large police departments in 2004, Mr

Futterman reports. Federal prosecutors are now investigating whether any commanders knew of the SOS debacle, but failed to stop it.

Breaking this code of silence might best begin with a strong new police superintendent. But the city is searching high and low for someone to replace Mr Cline. However, the next police chief, whoever he may be, cannot expect an overnight fix. Take Los Angeles. Since 1991, when police were taped beating Rodney King, the city has seen a wearingly repeating pattern of scandal and reform. (On October 9th investigators released their latest report, about police using excessive force against protesters and journalists in May.) If Los Angeles is any indication, Chicago's current wave of reform will not be its last.

4

Police Volunteers and Ethics

Carol Schmidt

Today, the public has become more actively involved with their local law enforcement agencies. With staffing shortages, departments have welcomed the extra resource that volunteers offer as a partial solution to some of their needs. (1) But, the increase in citizens volunteering with law enforcement agencies has added to the issues raised concerning those individuals who exercise authority and their ethical standards. How do law enforcement volunteers fit into this discussion?

The Clearwater, Florida, Police Department has had a successful volunteer program for several years and can offer some answers that may assist other agencies. Starting with about 12 steady volunteers nearly 10 years ago, the department now has 84 dedicated individuals who have proven their worth in countless ways. They have assisted citizens in potentially life-threatening situations, observed and reported crimes in progress that resulted in arrests, and assisted officers with many tasks. Based on the national average hourly value of a volunteer's time of $17.19 in 2003, (2) the department calculated that the 14,426 hours their volunteers contributed equated to $247,991. While this represents a remarkable demonstration of community support, it also illustrates the need for consistent oversight, comprehensive training, and well-developed guidelines that can help volunteers thrive in the law enforcement environment.

Advantages of a Volunteer Program

From an administrator's point of view, the use of volunteers offsets expenses without lowering the accomplishments of the agency. Volunteers do not replace sworn officers or any paid positions;

FBI Law Enforcement Bulletin. Reprinted by permission

instead, they enhance the quality of service that the organization can provide to its community.

Agencies use volunteers in numerous ways, from administrative tasks to assisting officers on the street. Administrative volunteers can help with data entry, filing, supply distribution, and many other office duties. Patrol volunteers can augment sworn officers in nonhazardous situations, such as parking enforcement, ordinance violations, traffic control, and special events.

From their viewpoint, volunteers gain a high sense of purpose by helping to keep their community safe and contributing to the agency's mission. They come to the law enforcement arena with different agendas and various backgrounds. Their reasons include looking toward a career in law enforcement, improving their promotional potential in their civilian jobs by volunteering, socializing with like-minded individuals, and giving back to their community. What they all have in common is a very high regard for law enforcement. Many other organizations need volunteers, but these citizens want to be involved in law enforcement. They also possess a variety of skills that they have acquired throughout their lives. Given adequate training, a friendly work environment, and a strong sense of belonging, volunteers can become extremely loyal and help the agency achieve its goals and objectives. To this end, they should reflect the organization's high professional standards.

Ethics and the Volunteer

Because volunteers can range in age from 18 to 90, they bring many different experiences, beliefs, and standards to the agency. Those with little life experience may not have a mature sense of ethics, whereas retired volunteers may have well-developed morals. This highlights the need for straightforward guidelines and a code of ethics adhered to by all personnel in the agency. Moreover, the department's culture will exemplify the ethical standards for volunteers.

Of course, law enforcement members have learned through advanced education and training what is necessary to be involved in the profession. They hold themselves to a higher standard of ethics than do most others in society. Volunteers have not had the same training, but their exposure to departmental personnel will influence how they conduct themselves. And, their training should bring them to the high caliber of ethics held by the agency.

Each department has a similar code of ethics for its members, and the same should hold true for volunteers. Differences in the performance of an officer compared with that of a volunteer will exist, but the rest of the code, such as accountability and responsibility, will apply. For example, volunteers must understand the importance of confidentiality and integrity. The public has the right to security and privacy; therefore, volunteers must remember to never improperly divulge information. In addition, they must behave in a manner that does not discredit the agency. As with officers, volunteers also should pursue the never-ending process of personal and professional development. This does not mean that they must sacrifice reflexivity as individuals. Their own personal ethics also will guide them.

Volunteers and the Agency

All members of the agency must deal consistently with volunteers. If favoritism occurs, animosity will develop among the volunteers and lessen the integrity of the organization in their eyes. Everyone should be governed by the same set of rules. Sometimes, rules have to bend, but, if they break, it will reflect on all of those connected with the agency.

It is important to know as much about the volunteer as possible to make sure that the person's ethics meet the agency's standards. During the processing of new volunteers, the department can obtain information from criminal histories, background checks, and interviews that will supply an initial idea of their ethical practices. During training, the agency should stress its moral standards, values, and ethics. As new volunteers associate with other volunteers and employees, the department can determine if their ethics will blend with those of the agency.

Volunteers do not have the same constant contact with the law enforcement organization that officers have, so what they see and hear on one occasion may influence their perceptions of officers and the way they respond to the agency's ethical standards. As volunteers have more contact with the members of the department, they will come to understand how the organization operates. This process may take a little longer than with paid employees because volunteers may have less frequent exposure to agency personnel.

Volunteers in Action

Once trained and issued a uniform, identification card, equipment, and vehicle, volunteers begin their foray into the community representing the agency. Sometimes, this leads volunteers to think that they have more authority than they do. Therefore, the department should monitor new volunteers for signs of their venturing beyond the guidelines. Examples would include stopping a vehicle for speeding or trying to move trespassers, rather than notifying officers of the situation. Such actions could compromise a volunteer's safety, a primary factor, but they also could generate complaints. Volunteers can curb such behavior by working in pairs and remembering that they serve as the "eyes and ears" of the agency.

Sometimes, volunteers do not realize that their actions could pose an ethical consideration. For example, they might show political preferences by wearing campaign buttons or conduct personal errands while patrolling. Being in uniform and stopping to buy alcohol on the way home, for instance, would not reflect well on the volunteer program or the agency. Although they may have done this many times while employed with other businesses, they must realize that they wear a uniform and represent the police department.

Volunteers must understand that they cannot use their positions for personal gain. They are expected to adhere to certain recognized principles and practices in the conduct of their public lives. They should know that their private lives also will be affected as they become part of the law enforcement family and the public sees them in uniform. Volunteers also should not accept gratuities, including food and beverages. (3) Sometimes, these temptations result from the interaction between society and the law enforcement community and not the individual volunteer. Specific, written guidelines can assist them in making decisions about their actions and in conducting themselves appropriately.

The law enforcement culture also should assume some of the responsibility for creating the environment that will either encourage or discourage ethical values. As they do law enforcement officers, citizens will scrutinize volunteers' actions, whether done in public or private. Volunteers must understand that they cannot abuse the authority of the uniform but have to display the highest degree of honesty, loyalty, and integrity to the agency and the community that they represent. It is paramount for all volunteers to realize that the program is only as effective as the individual performing the task. Instilling a sense of team spirit can help maintain the ethical standards of the agency whether volunteers work alone or in groups.

Conclusion

Law enforcement agencies should ensure that all members, paid employees or volunteers, are aware of the attitudes and actions expected of them. With this knowledge, all personnel will have a clear perspective of their responsibilities according to the ethical standards of their organizations.

The Clearwater, Florida, Police Department has had a successful volunteer program for nearly 10 years. By expecting the same exacting standards from its volunteers that it does from its paid personnel, the department has maintained the integrity of the profession while welcoming the support of these dedicated citizens who have enhanced the level of service it provides to the community it serves.

Code of Ethics of the Clearwater Police Department

* As a law enforcement officer, my fundamental duty is to serve mankind; to safeguard lives and property, to protect the innocent against deception, the weak against oppression or intimidation, and the peaceful against violence or disorder; and to respect the constitutional rights of all men to liberty, equality, and justice.
* I will keep my private life unsullied as an example to all; maintain courageous calm in the face of danger, scorn, or ridicule; develop self-restraint; and be constantly mindful of the welfare of others. Honest in thought and deed in both my personal and official life, I will be exemplary in obeying the laws of the land and the regulations of my department. Whatever I see or hear of a confidential nature or that is confided to me in my official capacity will be kept ever secret unless revelation is necessary in the performance of my duty.
* I will never act officiously or permit personal feelings, prejudices, animosities, or friendships to influence my decisions. With no compromise for crime and with relentless prosecution of criminals, I will enforce the law courteously and appropriately without fear or favor, malice or ill will, never employing unnecessary force or violence and never accepting gratuities.
* I recognize the badge of my office as a symbol of public faith, and I accept it as a public trust to be held so long as I am true to the ethics of the police service. I will constantly strive to achieve these objectives and ideals, dedicating myself before God to my chosen profession, law enforcement.

Endnotes

1. For additional information, see the Volunteers in Police Service (VIPS) Web site, http://www.policevolunteers.org.

2. http://www.independentsector.org

3. For additional information, see Mike White, "The Problem with Gratuities," FBI Law Enforcement Bulletin, July 2002, 20-23; Mike Corley, "Gratuities: There Is No Free Lunch," FBI Law Enforcement Bulletin, October 2005, 10-13.

5

Hollywood Inquiry Snares 3 More Officers

Three More Officers Are in Trouble in Hollywood, Accused of Leaking Information That Led to the Dismantling of an FBI Operation

Wanda J. Demarzo

The chief told a major, the major told a lieutenant and the lieutenant told a patrol officer -- who told another officer, who told another.

When all the whispering was done, a major FBI probe into corruption in the Hollywood Police Department was blown to bits.

Now, three months later, with four officers already facing prison sentences on drug trafficking charges, more heads are rolling.

Another three cops -- a major, a lieutenant and a patrol officer in one of Broward's largest police departments -- have been suspended and are under investigation by the FBI.

Relieved of duty Saturday in relation to the sting were Maj. Frank McGarry, Lt. Chuck Roberts and patrol officer Tammy Clyde. They are under investigation in connection with the leak, said police Captain Tony Rode.

McGarry, 45, has 24 years with the department; Roberts, 48, has 23 and Clyde, 38, has 16. None could be reached for comment Monday.

For Hollywood police Chief James Scarberry, it means defending his bruised department -- and perhaps even his own actions.

He commands a department with a history of corruption and allegations of criminal behavior -- including losing evidence, trading favors with prostitutes and planting drugs on suspects.

Scarberry declined to comment Monday on the latest problems, saying he would wait until all investigations are complete. The chief said he would be "disappointed" if one of his trusted staff blew the FBI probe.

But City Manager Cameron Benson said he wants his own review.

"I reserve the right to make sure we go as deep as we have to go to clean this up," said Benson.

Although Scarberry was the first to talk about the investigation, his job is not in jeopardy, Benson said.

Scarberry admitted he told his top commanders and some city leaders about the investigation but said he told them not to tell anyone. He defended his decision, saying the FBI told him to use his "discretion" in discussing the probe with others.

The federal investigation, dubbed "Operation Tarnished Badge," began in February 2004. The sting involved undercover FBI agents posing as members of a New York crime family who wanted protection for its South Florida operations.

But before the FBI agents could finish their investigation, the officers were tipped off, forcing the agency to shut down the operation. After learning they were the targets, two of the officers quickly filed their retirement papers and contacted attorneys.

Veteran officers Kevin Companion, 41; Stephen Harrison, 46; Thomas Simcox, 50; and Jeff Courtney, 52, already have pleaded guilty to conspiracy to possess with intent to distribute a multi-kilo load of heroin.

The original criminal complaint against the four detailed illegal activities including extortion, bribe-taking, dealing in stolen property, protecting a crooked high-stakes card game, cargo theft and transporting the load of heroin from Miami Beach to Oakwood Plaza in Hollywood for what the officers believed were mob-connected drug dealers.

They could face 10 years to life in prison but are hoping for a reduced sentence because they are cooperating with authorities. Sources said the leak moved from McGarry to Roberts to Clyde to Courtney.

On Friday, McGarry and his attorney, Hilliard Moldof, met with federal prosecutors, sources told The Miami Herald. Moldof refused to discuss his client or the investigation. The FBI, which had hoped to net other officers in the sting, was not happy with the outcome.

6

Civil Rights Group Faults How Police are Policed

Thomas J. Lueck.

A civil rights group yesterday criticized New York City's system of investigating police misconduct, charging that a civilian agency responsible for the task had failed to pursue complaints aggressively, and that punishment was too lenient when misconduct was established.

The New York Civil Liberties Union, which has long been critical of the agency, the Civilian Complaint Review Board, said that the board dismissed more than half its cases before fully investigating them, and that only about 5 percent of the cases were ultimately substantiated.

''Our analysis concludes that the civilian oversight system has failed,'' said Donna Lieberman, executive director of the civil rights group.

The report, which the civil liberties union said was based mainly on data made public by the board, says the board has failed to keep pace as the volume of civilian complaints about police misconduct, ranging from improper use of force to discourtesy, has risen by 86 percent since 2000.

Police Commissioner Raymond W. Kelly dismissed the findings yesterday, calling the analysis flawed. ''They are going to bash us every chance they get,'' he said of the civil rights group.

Mr. Kelly attributed the increase in citizen complaints to the city's 311 hot line, which went into operation in 2003, providing a convenient way to express displeasure with the police.

Andrew Case, a spokesman for the board, which employs 147 investigators, said its most recent records showed that 60 percent of the civilian complaints were being dismissed before they were completely investigated -- but only because those who made those complaints decided not to follow through. He said none of those cases would have been dropped if those who had complained, mainly through calls to 311, had been willing to appear and make formal statements at the board's office in Lower Manhattan, as city rules dictate.

And Franklin H. Stone, the chairwoman of the board, which was established as an oversight agency outside the Police Department in 1992, said that the board had fulfilled its City Charter mission ''extraordinarily well.''

The civil rights group said the system of police conduct review was rife with problems resulting from obfuscation by the police, and a failure by the board and its staff to challenge the authority of top police officials.

Among its recommendations were that the city appoint a new inspector general to monitor the conduct of the police and the performance of the Civilian Complaint Review Board. And it criticized the current system of prosecuting officers when the board substantiates civilian cases. A legal unit of the Police Department now handles the prosecutions; the civil rights group suggested having prosecutors outside the department take the cases.

''The commissioner blatantly disregards C.C.R.B. recommendations time and time again,'' Ms. Lieberman said. ''It is ironic that a Police Department that pursues zero tolerance on the streets does not pursue zero tolerance in its own ranks.''

The report said that investigators for the board were often handicapped by the police's delays in turning over documents or evidence, and that officers named in complaints frequently failed to show up for interviews.

When discipline of officers is ordered by the department, it rarely fits the severity of their misconduct, the group said. ''In recent years, there has been a radically more lenient policy,'' said Robert A. Perry, an analyst for the civil rights group who was in charge of the study released yesterday. In most cases, the discipline involves having a description of the officer's misconduct included in his or her personnel file, verbal reprimands from the precinct commanders, or, in more serious cases, suspensions or lost vacation days.

The report found that the proportion of cases in which officers received the lightest penalty -- a note in the file -- had risen to 74 percent in 2006 from less than 25 percent in 2000. In the same period, it said, the proportion of officers who were suspended or lost vacation days dropped to 5 percent from 34 percent.

Mr. Case said some of the criticisms raised in the report, including the one about lenient discipline, had been made by the board itself. The board ''has reported publicly and often on the decreasing severity of the department's discipline,'' he said.

Questions about the board's recommendations were referred by a spokeswoman for the mayor to Mr. Case. He said appointing a new inspector general might have little impact.

''At what point do you stop and say the people that are in place need to get the issues resolved,'' he said.

Paul J. Browne, a police spokesman, said the report yesterday ignored the resources being committed to monitoring the conduct of officers in cooperation with the Civilian Complaint Review Board and through the police internal affairs unit.

''True to form, the N.Y.C.L.U. has distorted or ignored the facts to reach its predetermined conclusions,'' Mr. Browne said. He said about 1,000 members of the department were assigned to internal investigations, roughly the same number assigned to counterterrorism and intelligence.

7

Prosecutors Say Corruption in Atlanta Police Dept. is Widespread

Shaila Dewan, Brenda Goodman

After the fatal police shooting of an elderly woman in a botched drug raid, the United States attorney here said Thursday that prosecutors were investigating a ''culture of misconduct'' in the Atlanta Police Department.

In court documents, prosecutors said Atlanta police officers regularly lied to obtain search warrants and fabricated documentation of drug purchases, as they had when they raided the home of the woman, Kathryn Johnston, in November, killing her in a hail of bullets.

Narcotics officers have admitted to planting marijuana in Ms. Johnston's home after her death and submitting as evidence cocaine they falsely claimed had been bought at her house, according to the court filings.

Two of the three officers indicted in the shooting, Gregg Junnier and Jason R. Smith, pleaded guilty on Thursday to state charges including involuntary manslaughter and federal charges of conspiracy to violate Ms. Johnston's civil rights.

''Former officers Junnier and Smith will also help us continue our very active ongoing investigation into just how wide the culture of misconduct that led to this tragedy extends within the Atlanta Police Department,'' said David Nahmias, the United States attorney.

Asked how widespread such practices might be, Mr. Nahmias said investigators were looking at narcotics officers, officers who had once served in the narcotics unit and ''officers that had never been in that unit but may have adopted that practice.''

The investigation has already led to scrutiny of criminal cases involving the indicted officers and others who may have used similar tactics. Paul Howard, the Fulton County district attorney, said his office was reviewing at least 100 cases involving the three officers, including 10 in which defendants were in jail.

If they continue to cooperate, Mr. Junnier, who retired after the shooting, faces a minimum of 10 years in prison and Mr. Smith, who resigned Thursday, faces 12 years.

The third officer, Arthur Tesler, declined a plea deal. He was indicted on charges of violation of oath by a public officer, making false statements and false imprisonment under color of legal process.

Mr. Tesler's lawyer, John Garland, said his client was following his training when he put false claims in an affidavit.

Mr. Nahmias took a moment to dwell on what he said was the unusual nature of the officers' offenses.

''The officers charged today were not corrupt in the sense that we have seen before,'' he said. ''They are not accused of seeking payoffs or trying to rob drug dealers or trying to protect gang members. Their goal was to arrest drug dealers and seize illegal drugs, and that's what we want our police officers to do for our community.

''But these officers pursued that goal by corrupting the justice system, because when it was hard to do their job the way the Constitution requires, they let the ends justify their means.''

Mr. Nahmias said the statement in the plea agreement that officers cut corners in order to ''be considered productive officers and to meet A.P.D.'s performance targets'' reflected their perception of the department's expectations.

The police chief, Richard Pennington, said that officers were not trained to lie and that they had no performance quotas. Two weeks ago, he announced changes to the narcotics squad, including increasing the unit's size and more careful reviews of requests for so-called no-knock warrants like the one served on Ms. Johnston's home.

''Let me assure you, if we find out any other officers have been involved in such egregious acts, they will be dealt with just as sternly as these other officers have been,'' said Chief Pennington, who after the shooting asked for a review by the Federal Bureau of Investigation. ''I assure you that we will not tolerate any officers violating the law and mistreating our citizens in this city.''

The death of Ms. Johnston, whose age is listed variously as 88 or 92, outraged Atlantans, brought simmering discontent with police conduct toward residents to a boil and led to the creation of a civilian review board for the Police Department.

The day she was killed, narcotics officers said, they arrested a drug dealer who said he could tell them where to recover a kilogram of cocaine, and pointed out Ms. Johnston's modest green-trimmed house at 933 Neal Street.

Instead of hiring an informant to try to buy drugs at the house, the officers filed for a search warrant, claiming that drugs had been bought there from a man named Sam. Because they falsely claimed that the house was equipped with surveillance equipment, they got a no-knock warrant that allowed them to break down the front door.

First, according to court papers, they pried off the burglar bars and began to ram open the door. Ms. Johnston, who lived alone, fired a single shot from a .38-caliber revolver through the front door and the officers fired back, killing her.

After the shooting, they handcuffed her and searched the house, finding no drugs.

''She was without question an innocent civilian who was caught in the worst circumstance imaginable,'' Mr. Howard, the district attorney, said at a news conference on Thursday. ''When we learned of her death, all of us imagined our own mothers and our own grandmothers in her place, and the thought made us shudder.''

When no drugs were found, the cover-up began in earnest, according to court papers.

Officer Smith planted three bags of marijuana, which had been recovered earlier in the day in an unrelated search, in the basement. He called a confidential informant and instructed him to pretend he had made the drug buy described in the affidavit for the search warrant.

The three officers, Mr. Junnier, Mr. Smith and Officer Tesler met to concoct a story before talking with homicide detectives, the court filings say.

Though the three met several more times, prosecutors said, Mr. Junnier admitted the truth in his first interview with F.B.I. agents. Mr. Smith at first lied about his role, but later admitted to the conspiracy.

8

Law Enforcement Ethics Do Not Begin When You Pin on the Badge

Norman Stephens

In every person's life, there are particular dates that can be mentally retrieved in a moment's notice. September 11, 2001, immediately comes to mind. December 7, 1941, is a day "that will live in infamy," and July 4, 1776, is the day the United States gained its independence. Dates of national importance are not the only ones we remember. The birth of a child, the death of a parent, the anniversary of our marriage are just as likely to spark our recollection. For those blessed to be police officers, the day they first recited the police code of ethics can compete with each of these dates.

Over the years, I have had the opportunity to lecture future law enforcement officers in the classrooms of colleges and universities--young men and women making the decision to serve even though they easily could have chosen a safer, more lucrative career path. I also have had the misfortune to counsel equally bright and ambitious young people who, due to poor decision making, will never be afforded the honor of pinning on the badge. Because of those uncomfortable moments, I realized that the characteristics associated with the police code of ethics does not begin the day a person becomes a police officer; it must become a part of the future officer's life as early as teenage years.

Few professions demand as much moral fiber as policing. Indiscretions, easily overlooked in other political arenas, bring shame and mistrust in the field of law enforcement. There is little more ethical expectation of religious leaders than of police officers. The International Association of Chiefs of Police published the Law Enforcement Code of Ethics as a reminder to all those in law enforcement of their commitment to the public they serve. Although the code is over 250 words in length, for the purpose of brevity, I focus on fewer than 65. "I will keep my private life unsullied as an example to all ... maintain courageous calm in the face of danger, scorn, or ridicule; develop self-restraint; and be constantly mindful of the welfare of others. Honest in thought and deed both in my personal and official life, I will be exemplary in obeying the law and the regulations of my department."

Now, more than ever, police administrators are not willing to hire average applicants. No longer is simply being bigger, stronger, and tougher a prerequisite for employment. Chiefs, faced with greater public scrutiny and potential civil liability, search for more gifted employees. Seldom will a police administrator overlook deficiencies in an applicant when a potential candidate waiting in the wings may have less baggage. The initial financial outlay required to hire, educate, and outfit an officer has dramatically reduced an organization's desire to give a person a tryout. Instead, there is a renewed interest to hire the right person the first time.

Those who dream of a career in law enforcement often find themselves either apologizing, rationalizing, or, worse yet, misleading potential employers about their past indiscretions. Theodore Roosevelt once said, "No man can lead a public career really worth leading, no man can act with rugged independence in serious crises, nor strike at great abuses, nor afford to make powerful and unscrupulous foes, if he is himself vulnerable in his private character." Inasmuch as all people will have to answer for themselves on judgment day, that day begins for those applying to become a police officer when they fill out the application for employment. Throughout this process, their past will be scrutinized by a number of people. If the background investigation is done correctly, there should be very little about the person that the future employer is not aware. It is difficult for people to hide their past. In Character and Cops, Edwin Delattre explains the need for police agencies to hire officers of the highest ethical character.

The mission of policing can safely be entrusted only to those who grasp what is morally important and who respect integrity. Without this kind of personal character in police, no set of codes or rules or laws can safeguard that mission from the ravages of police misconduct. No one need choose to be a police officer or to bear the public trust; but those who do so--no matter how naively and no matter how misguided their original expectations--must acquire the excellence of character necessary to live up to it.

Going away to college is traditionally the initial step toward adulthood for many young people. For the first time in their lives, the clear-cut boundaries established by their parents become blurred. Outside influences, extracurricular activities, and expendable income, coupled with the desire to experience college life, is a persuasive cocktail ready for consumption. No longer is an immediate adult influence poised to run interference on their secular destination. College life, this seemingly innocent rite of passage that breeds opportunity toward immediate short-term gratification, has eventually proven the ruin of many able-bodied recruits. "If it feels good, do it."; "Who is going to know?"; "It's only marijuana."; and "You're an adult now." These are only a few things college students say to encourage and condone each other's actions. Regrettably, the seemingly innocent participation of recreational drugs in college will serve as a stumbling block in the student's path toward a career in law enforcement.

Historically, as students approach their senior year, they begin to concentrate more on the future than the immediate. It is, generally, at this time that I will be approached and questioned about the penalty regarding past indiscretions. As the standards for employment are explained, the feeling of disappointment is nearly palpable. Perhaps, for the first time, the young adults realize they are accountable for their past, and it is certainly going to affect their future.

The purpose of this speech is not intended to direct college students toward a puritan lifestyle. It is not an effort to diminish the college experience or to impart my values on the listener. What it is intended to do is to serve as a wake-up call, a gentle reminder that for every decision you make, you are accountable. It is no one else's fault. There is no other to shift the blame to. For those who desire a career in law enforcement, the past is not the past. It is not something to learn from and then move on. The excuse, "I was young and dumb," holds no weight. You are an adult. You are liable. Your past will be revealed.

In closing, the founder of the Methodist Church, John Wesley, said it best, "Do all the good you can, by all the means you can, in all the ways you can, in all the places you can, at all the times you can, to all the people you can, as long as you can." The day you are administered the law enforcement code of ethics should serve as a reminder, not as a challenge.

Deputy Chief Stephens serves with the Broken Arrow, Oklahoma, Police Department.

Chapter 2

The Courtroom Workgroup

Ethics in the System

1

Looking Anew At Campaign Cash And Elected Judges

Adam Liptak

Vernon Valentine Palmer, a law professor at Tulane University in New Orleans, could not understand how justices of the Louisiana Supreme Court could routinely hear cases involving people who had given them campaign contributions. It seemed to him a raw and simple conflict of interest.

So he wrote polite letters to each of the seven justices, urging them to adopt a rule that would make disqualification mandatory in those cases.

Six months passed without a single response, and he wrote again. ''I used seven more stamps,'' he said, ''and I still got no reply.''

Professor Palmer is a senior member of the Tulane law faculty and the director of its European legal studies program. He is not an expert on judicial ethics, but he knows a thing or two about the rule of law.

Peeved, he decided to take a closer look at the Louisiana Supreme Court. He recruited John Levendis, an economics professor at Loyola University in New Orleans, to help with the statistics, along with a half-dozen law students to crunch numbers and code cases. Their conclusions, to be published next month in The Tulane Law Review, are not pretty.

In nearly half of the cases they reviewed, over a 14-year period ended in 2006, a litigant or lawyer had contributed to at least one justice, sometimes recently and sometimes long before. On average, justices voted in favor of their contributors 65 percent of the time, and two of the justices did so 80 percent of the time.

The conventional response to such findings is that they do not prove much.

Judges do not change their votes in response to contributions, the argument goes. Rather, contributors support judges whose legal philosophies they find congenial and, incidentally, sometimes benefit when their judges apply those philosophies in a principled and consistent way that just happens to benefit them.

You may think that is a distinction without a difference, which is why you do not teach judicial ethics.

Professor Palmer was, in any event, able to address that objection by asking several additional questions.

He looked first at cases in which no one involved in the lawsuit had ever made a contribution, before or after the suit was filed, to establish a baseline. Some judges tended to vote for plaintiffs, others for defendants.

Justice John L. Weimer, for instance, was slightly pro-defendant in cases where neither side had given him contributions, voting for plaintiffs 47 percent of the time. But in cases where he received money from the defense side (or more money from the defense when both sides gave money), he voted for the plaintiffs only 25 percent of the time. In cases where the money from the plaintiffs' side dominated, on the other hand, he voted for the plaintiffs 90 percent of the time. That is quite a swing.

"It is the donation, not the underlying philosophical orientation, that appears to account for the voting outcome," Professor Palmer said.

Larger contributions had larger effects, the study found. Justice Catherine D. Kimball was 30 percent more likely to vote for a defendant with each additional $1,000 donation. The effect was even more pronounced for Justice Weimer, who was 300 percent more likely to do so.

"The greater the size of the contribution," Professor Palmer said, "the greater the odds of favorable outcomes."

A similar study of the Ohio Supreme Court conducted by The New York Times in 2006 continues to echo in that state. It appeared about a year after an appeals court there threw out a $212 million jury verdict in a case involving a business dispute between two companies, and it caused the lawyers on the losing side to take a look at who had contributed to the campaign of the judge who wrote the decision. It turned out that the judge, William G. Batchelder, had received a lot of money from Robert Meyerson, the chief executive of the company on the winning side, the Telxon Corporation.

The lawyers for the company on the losing side, Smart Media, asked for a rehearing and got one, sort of. In November, a substitute panel of appeals court judges refused to undo the earlier decision, saying there was no procedure to allow that. Judge Robert Nader, dissenting, could barely contain his disbelief, saying the initial decision was infected by ''approximately $1 million in contributions from a very financially interested individual'' to Judge Batchelder, a Republican, and to the local Republican Party.

This was, Judge Nader wrote, ''a classic scenario giving rise to every nuance of political influence in our courts which calls for self-disqualification.''

The case is now before the Ohio Supreme Court. Mr. Meyerson, the executive, has given money to two of its justices as well.

A couple of weeks ago, the United States Supreme Courtsaid the Constitution had nothing to say about the way New York elects its judges. But several justices went out of their way to question the practice of electing judges. Justices Anthony M. Kennedy and Stephen G. Breyer said, for instance, that campaign fund-raising in judicial elections might be at odds ''with the perception and the reality of judicial independence and judicial excellence.''

But you do not have to do away with elections and or even fund-raising to make a drastic improvement in the quality of justice in state courts around the nation. All you need to do is listen to Professor Palmer. If a judge has taken money from a litigant or a lawyer, Professor Palmer says, the judge has no business ruling on that person's case.

CAPTION(S)

CHART: MONEY AND JUDICIAL RULINGS: According to a study of 181 court cases from March 1992 to July 2006, Louisiana Supreme Court justices tended to vote in favor of their campaign contributors. (Source: Vernon Valentine Palmer and John Levendis, Tulane Law Review)

2

Charged PA Judge to Seek 2nd Term

Jason Cato

A state appeals judge accused of swindling two insurance companies out of more than $400,000 vowed Thursday to press on with the campaign to keep his Superior Court seat, despite a call to resign by the head of the state Democratic Party.

A federal grand jury this week indicted Michael T. Joyce, a Republican from Erie, on nine counts of mail fraud and money laundering. He proclaimed his innocence yesterday and said he plans to seek another 10-year term in November.

"I have spent almost 23 years on the bench and have instructed hundreds of juries that in the United States, one is presumed innocent until proven guilty," Joyce, 58, said in a statement. "Just because there is a charge does not mean an actual crime has occurred."

The Administrative Office for Pennsylvania Courts could determine as early as today how the charges will impact Joyce's job status, a spokesman said.

"We will monitor the federal case closely," said Joseph Massa, chief counsel of the state Judicial Conduct Board.

Although state Republican Party officials were unavailable for comment, T.J. Rooney, chairman of the state Democratic Party, said Joyce should do the "honorable thing" and step down.

"It is absolutely incomprehensible to me as to how a judge would subject himself to this kind of negative publicity and still have the audacity to ask to serve the public, rather than excuse himself from the process and demonstrating humility and remorse," Rooney said in a statement.

Prosecutors accuse Joyce of defrauding the insurance companies after a minor car crash in August 2001. A year later, he submitted claims in which he said pain from the wreck kept him from playing golf and performing other physical activities.

Prosecutors, however, say from May to July 2002, Joyce submitted golf score cards to the Western Pennsylvania Golf Association to maintain his handicap. Among the nine rounds he submitted, two were played in Runaway Bay, Jamaica -- where he also went scuba diving in January 2002, prosecutors said.

The judge obtained a pilot's license during this time period, became recertified as a scuba instructor and worked out at a private gym, the indictment states. Joyce used the insurance money to buy property, a Harley-Davidson motorcycle and partial ownership in a Cessna airplane, all of which the government wants to seize, according to the indictment.

3

ATLA Members' Code of Conduct

Association of Trial Lawyers of America

1. No ATLA member shall personally, or through a representative, contact any party, or an aggrieved survivor, in an attempt to solicit a potential client when there has been no request for such contact from the injured party, an aggrieved survivor, or a relative of either, or the injured parties' union representative.

2. No ATLA member shall go to the scene of an event which caused injury unless requested to do so by an interested party, an aggrieved survivor, a relative of either, or by an attorney representing an injured party or survivor.

3. No ATLA member shall initiate a television appearance or initiate any comment to any news media concerning an event causing injury within 10 days of the event unless the member forgoes any financial return from the compensation of those injured or killed, provided, however, that an individual designated by a bar association to state the official position of such bar association may initiate such media contact to communicate such position.

4. No ATLA member shall personally, or through an associate attorney, file a complaint with a specific ad damnum amount unless required by local rules of court. If such amount is stated, it shall be based upon good faith evaluation of facts which the member can demonstrate.

5. No ATLA member shall personally, or through a representative, make representations of trial experience or past results of litigation either of which is in any way false or misleading.

Trial, Dec 2005 v41 i13 p70(1)
ATLA members' code of conduct.(Association of Trial Lawyers of America)

6. No ATLA member shall personally, or through a representative, initiate personal contact with a potential client (who is not a client, former client, relative or close personal friend of the attorney) for the purpose of advising that individual of the possibility of an unrecognized legal claim for damages unless the member forgoes any financial interest in the compensation of the injured party.

7. No ATLA member shall file or maintain a frivolous suit, issue, or position. However, no ATLA member should refrain from urging or arguing any suit, issue, or position that he believes in good faith to have merit.

8. The ATLA Board of Governors has condemned attorneys or legal clinics who advertise for clients in personal injury cases and who have no intention of handling the cases themselves, but do so for the sole purpose of brokering the case to other attorneys. Any ATLA member who enters a contract of representation on behalf of a claimant shall, at the time of retention, fully advise the client, in writing, of all relationships with other attorneys who will be involved in the presentation, the role each attorney shall play, and the proposed division of fees among them. The client shall also be promptly advised of all changes affecting the representation.

9. No ATLA member shall knowingly accept a referral from a person, whether an ATLA member or not, who obtained the representation by conduct which this code prohibits.

4

Attorney-Client Privilege Keeps Wrong Man in Prison

Maurice Possley

For a quarter of a century, defense lawyers Dale Coventry and Jamie Kunz were bound by the rules of law to hold onto a secret that now could mean freedom for a man serving a life sentence for murder.

The secret _ memorialized on a notarized affidavit that they locked in a metal box _ was that their client, Andrew Wilson, admitted that he shotgunned to death a security guard at a McDonald's restaurant on Chicago's South Side in January 1982.

Bound to silence by attorney-client privilege, Kunz and Coventry could do nothing as another man, Alton Logan, 54, was tried and convicted instead.

The two lawyers testified in court last week that they were bound by the attorney-client privilege and Wilson's admonition that they only reveal his admission after his death. Wilson, who was serving a life sentence for the murders of two Chicago police officers, died of natural causes Nov. 19.

Their testimony sets the stage for what could be a legal battle over the admission of the secret in court.

"The prosecution should put on the white hat and get this poor innocent man out," Coventry said Friday.

Assistant Illinois Atty. Gen. Richard Schwind, who is representing the state, declined to comment because the case is pending.

Coventry and Kunz both recounted separately how they had been haunted over the years by knowing that they had evidence of Logan's innocence, but could not legally disclose it until Wilson died.

"It was a relief," said Kunz, 70. "Oh my God, I have been wanting this. I have considered this to be the truth. I have been wanting this to come out for years. I don't know anything about Alton Logan. It hurts to know somebody is in prison all these years and is innocent."

The saga began with the Jan. 11, 1982, robbery at the McDonald's at 11421 S. Halsted St., where security guard Lloyd Wycliffe was killed by a shotgun blast and another security guard, Alvin Thompson, was wounded. The gunmen got no money, but stole the guards' handguns.

On Feb. 5, 1982, Edgar Hope was arrested after he fatally shot one police officer and wounded another on a CTA bus on East 79th Street. He was carrying the gun taken from Thompson at the McDonald's.

Two days later, on Feb. 7, 1982, Logan was arrested and, along with Hope, charged with robbery and murder in the McDonald's case, based on the testimony of witnesses who said he shotgunned Wycliffe.

The ink was barely dry on the charges when, on Feb. 9, Chicago police officers William Fahey and Richard O'Brien were shot dead near 8500 S. Morgan St. Their guns were taken. The crime triggered a massive search for Andrew Wilson and his brother, Jackie.

On Feb. 13, police raided a beauty parlor where they believed Andrew Wilson had been hiding. While they did not find Wilson, they did find the revolvers belonging to Fahey and O'Brien, as well as a shotgun. Firearms tests linked the shotgun to a shotgun shell found at the McDonald's restaurant, according to court records.

But with two men already charged in the McDonald's shootings, which witnesses said involved only two gunmen, authorities never charged Wilson in that case.

The arrest of the Wilson brothers for the murder of the two police officers has become infamous in Chicago because the Wilsons asserted that Chicago Police Cmdr. Jon Burge and some of his detectives tortured them during questioning. Those assertions were later proved and ultimately led to the department firing Burge and further allegations by scores of defendants that they were tortured by Burge or his detectives.

Coventry and Kunz, both then assistant Cook County public defenders, were assigned to be Andrew Wilson's lawyers. In March, just a few weeks later, Marc Miller, then the attorney defending Edgar Hope, came to Kunz and Coventry to say that his client was contending that Logan was innocent.

"Hope said that (Logan) had nothing to do with the McDonald's case, and that it was Andrew Wilson who was with him and Andrew Wilson who shotgunned the security guard," Kunz said.

Coventry and Kunz said they confronted Wilson with Hope's claim.

"He kind of chuckled over the fact that someone else was charged with something he did," Coventry, 64, recalled.

Kunz said, "Wilson said, `Yeah' or `Uh-huh,' nodded, grinned, and said, `That was me.'"

At the time, the lawyers were bound by attorney ethics not to disclose Wilson's statement, but he said they could reveal it after his death. Under the legal principle of attorney-client privilege, conversations between a client and his lawyer are almost always confidential, unless the client agrees to disclose them.

On March 17, 1982, Coventry and Kunz drew up an affidavit:

"I have obtained information through privileged sources that a man named Alton Logan who was charged with the fatal shooting of Lloyd Wickliffe (sic) at on or about 11 Jan. 82 is in fact not responsible for that shooting that in fact another person was responsible."

Each lawyer signed it, as did a witness and a notary public. Then they sealed it in a metal box.

"We were freaked out because it was really volatile and because the state was seeking the death penalty against Logan," said Coventry, who has kept the box ever since.

Kunz said they prepared the document "so that if we were ever able to speak up, no one could say we were just making this up now."

Assistant Cook County public defender Harold Winston, who is currently representing Logan in a motion for a new trial, said that he had heard rumors for years that Kunz and Coventry had information about Wilson's involvement in the McDonald's case. After Wilson died, he reached out to Kunz.

Kunz contacted Coventry, who found the metal box and unsealed the envelope. Both were summoned to court Jan. 11, where Criminal Court Judge James Schreier ruled that they could reveal the conversation with Wilson and the contents of the affidavit. After hearing their testimony, the judge asked for legal briefs on the admissibility of Wilson's statement that he _ not Logan _ killed the McDonald's guard.

Richard Kling, the attorney for Hope who has been seeking to prove Hope is innocent, likely will oppose any statement that could be used against his client. But he also said, "I admire Jamie

Kunz and Dale Coventry for coming forward as soon as they were able with a document showing that the wrong man was convicted."

Hope and Logan were convicted of the McDonald's case and Hope was sentenced to death. Logan was sentenced to life in prison.

Jack Rimland, who defended Logan at that trial, said he always believed Andrew Wilson had killed the security guard. "Logan told me all along that he didn't do it," Rimland said. "I would like to see the guy get justice."

5

The Reality of Political Prisoners in the United States

What September 11 Taught Us About Defending Them

Jill Sofiyah Elijah

Defending the "unpopular client," the client who has been targeted by the government as a terrorist, a cop killer, a bank robber, a revolutionary, or the "the sole white member of the Black Liberation Army" does not get you nominated to the list of America's 100 Most Influential Lawyers. Nonetheless, the Constitution and accepted ethical and criminal procedure norms guarantee that every defendant is entitled to legal counsel and zealous advocacy.

That is what is taught in law school, but is that what is meant? Recent legislation has raised serious doubts as to whether we can continue to take these principles for granted. How else can we explain the recent unprecedented arrest and indictment of New York lawyer, Lynn Stewart, a zealous advocate who is well respected among members of the bar and bench? (1) Ms. Stewart has represented numerous "unpopular" clients. Some of them have clear political ideologies, such as David Gilbert, who was charged as a former member of the Weather Underground with the 1981 Brinks armored car robbery in Nyack, New York. Also included were Bilal Sunni-Ali, a member of the Republic of New Africa, who was charged in the 1981 Brinks case in a federal prosecution and Richard Williams, who was alleged to have conspired with members of the Ohio 7 to blow up several military buildings and offices of major corporations. Gilbert and Williams were convicted in 1983 and 1986, respectively, and remain incarcerated today as political prisoners.

Sunni-Ali was acquitted in an emotional and political upset for the U.S. Attorney's Office for the Southern District of New York. At that time, none other than Rudolph Giuliani directed the office. Ms. Stewart has been a thorn in the side of prosecutors for over two decades. It seems that the time for revenge has arrived.

No wonder the U.S. attorney general boldly announced at a press conference following her arraignment that the federal government has been monitoring conversations between Stewart and her client, Sheikh Omar Abdel-Rahman, from at least as far back as May 2000. Even the most conservative observer would concede that the U.S. Patriot Act was not signed into law until October 26, 2001. A scrupulous review of its provisions will reveal no specific reference to monitoring of attorney-client communications. Upon what authority did the government rely in determining that it could monitor undisputed attorney-client communications in May 2000? Attorney General John Ashcroft shamelessly admitted that Ms. Stewart's conversations with her client were surreptitiously wiretapped during a prison visit that took place two years ago.

Before October 30, 2001, the Bureau of Prisons regulations on institutional management authorized the Bureau to impose special administrative measures with respect to specified inmates. These administrative measures had to be based on information provided by senior intelligence or law enforcement officials, where it was determined to be necessary to prevent the dissemination either of classified information that could endanger the national security or of other information that could lead to acts of violence and terrorism. (2) However, those regulations did not contemplate that communications between an inmate and his or her attorney would be subject to the usual rules for monitoring of inmate communications.

On October 30, 2001, the Department of Justice instituted new regulations that amended certain key provisions. Beyond extending the time during which a prisoner could be subjected to special administrative measures from 120 days to up to one year, the new regulations provide,

> d) In any case where the Attorney General specifically so orders, based on information from the head of a federal law enforcement or intelligence agency that reasonable suspicion exists to believe that a particular inmate may use communications with attorneys or their agents to further or facilitate acts of terrorism, the Director, Bureau of Prisons, shall, in addition to the special administrative measures imposed under paragraph (a) of this section, provide appropriate procedures for the monitoring or review of communications between that inmate and attorneys' agents who are traditionally covered by the attorney-client

> privilege, for the purpose of deterring future acts that could result in death or serious bodily injury to persons, or substantial damage to property that would entail the risk of death or serious bodily injury to persons. (3)

It is alleged inter alia in the federal indictment that Ms. Stewart violated the Special Administrative Measure imposed on Sheik Omar Abdel-Rahman since 1997 by facilitating communications between him and members of what the FBI has dubbed the Islamic Group. (4) The Islamic Group is described in the indictment as an "international terrorist group dedicated to opposing nations, governments, institutions and individuals that did not share [its] radical interpretation of Islamic law." The basis for the government's indictment of Stewart is the apparent illegal monitoring of her communications with her client. Although the October 2001 amendments to the Bureau of Prisons may permit the government's conduct under limited conditions now, there appears to be no authority for their actions before that date.

Nevertheless, history is instructive here. In 1991, around the time that Lynne Stewart was having her difficulties with the Manhattan D.A.'s office, attorney Linda Backiel was being targeted by the U.S. attorney's office in Philadelphia for her refusal to testify before a federal grand jury about communications she had had with Elizabeth Ann Duke, a client who was believed to have jumped bail. Ms. Duke was an admitted revolutionary who had been indicted on weapons and explosives charges. Ms. Backiel, like Ms. Stewart, had represented a number of "politically unpopular" clients such as Kathy Boudin, who was charged as a member of the Weather Underground with the 1981 Brinks armored car robbery in Nyack, New York, and Antonio Camacho Negron, who was charged with conspiracy in the 1983 Wells Fargo $7.1 million dollar robbery in West Hartford, Connecticut. Mr. Camacho was a Puerto Rican independentista and was alleged to be a member of Los Macheteros. Ms. Backiel spent six months in jail for civil contempt before the grand jury disbanded.

As the nation begins to accept greater infringements on civil liberties, it seems that lawyers are among the first to feel the intrusion into their profession. Indeed, Ms. Stewart believes that she is being used as an example to deter others from representing controversial figures and causes.

How do we explain the fact that the Arabic-speaking, court-certified interpreter was also indicted with Ms. Stewart? What was his crime? Translating documents into English for Ms. Stewart and her client? Is an interpreter who is hired to aid the attorney and client in their communications responsible for screening the things he is asked to interpret? If the interpreter's prosecution is allowed to go forward, it will be nearly impossible for attorneys representing "unpopular" clients to hire translators for them during prison visits and phone calls. There seems to be no limit to the possible abuses. The net has been cast far too wide. Many would argue that the net should not have been cast at all.

The message is clear. Attorneys who believe that they are obliged to follow the Code of Professional Responsibility and "not decline representation because a client or a cause is unpopular or community reaction is adverse" (5) are at risk of being targeted for character assassination and prosecuted to the full extent of, and in some instances, beyond the law.

NOTES

1. Sadly, this is not the first time Ms. Stewart has been used as a test case by the government in unprecedented interference in the attorney-client relationship. Back in 1989, the Manhattan District Attorney's office, led by Robert Morgenthau, attempted to undermine Ms. Stewart's representation of her client, Dominick Maldonado, by having unauthorized communications with him and convincing him to cooperate. This lead him to participate in a scheme concocted by the D.A.'s office that ultimately led to felony charges being lodged against Ms. Stewart for contempt of court. She refused to testify before a grand jury investigating the source and amount of funds paid to her and other lawyers in the case. Mr. Maldonado was charged with participation in a heroin ring. The charges against Ms. Stewart were ultimately reduced. Her client committed suicide after being sentenced to 100 years, realizing that he had been misled and used as a pawn to destroy her career.

2. 28 CFR Parts 500 and 501.

3. (1) The certification by the Attorney General under this paragraph (d) shall be in addition to any findings or determinations relating to the need for the imposition of other special administrative measures as provided in paragraph (a) of this section, but may be incorporated into the same document.

(2) Except in the case of prior court authorization, the Director, Bureau of Prisons, shall provide written notice to the inmate and to the attorneys involved, prior to the initiation of any monitoring or review under this paragraph (d). The notice shall explain:

(i) That, notwithstanding the provisions of part 540 of this chapter or other rules, all communications between the

inmate and attorneys may be monitored, to the extent determined to be reasonably necessary for the purpose of deterring future acts of violence or terrorism;
(ii) That communications between the inmate and attorneys or their agents are not protected by the attorney-client privilege if they would facilitate criminal acts or a conspiracy to commit criminal acts, or if those communications are not related to the seeking or providing or legal advice.

(3) The Director, Bureau of Prisons, with the approval of the Assistant Attorney General for the Criminal Division, shall employ appropriate procedures to ensure that all attorney-client communications are reviewed for privilege claims and that any properly privileged materials (including, but not limited to, recordings of privileged communications) are not retained during the course of the monitoring. To protect the attorney-client privilege and to ensure that the investigation is not compromised by exposure to privileged material relating to the investigation or to defense strategy, a privilege team shall be designated, consisting of individuals not involved in the underlying investigation. The monitoring shall be conducted pursuant to procedures designed to minimize the intrusion into privileged material or conversations. Except in cases where the person in charge of the privilege team determines that acts of violence or terrorism are imminent, the privilege team shall not disclose any information unless and until such disclosure has been approved by a federal judge.

4. 02 Crim. 395 SDNY Paragraph 16.

5. The ABA Model Code, EC 2-27 states that regardless of personal feelings, “a lawyer should not decline representation because a client or cause is unpopular or community reaction is adverse.”

JILL SOFFIYAH ELIJAH serves as a clinical instructor with Harvard Law School’s Criminal Justice Institute (302 Austin Hall, Cambridge, MA 02138; e-mail: jelijah@law.harvard.edu), after resigning from her position as the Director of the Defender Clinic at the City University of New York School of Law. Over the past 18 years, she has represented numerous political prisoners and social activists. The views and opinions expressed herein are solely those of the author and are not necessarily reflective of the position held by Harvard Law School or the Criminal Justice Institute.

6

No Gatekeeper of Justice

Bennett L. Gershman, Joel Cohen

More than any other recent criminal case, the prosecution of three Duke University lacrosse players for the rape of a young woman at a party has exposed to a national audience an unbridled abuse of prosecutorial power.

From the outset, the Durham County, N.C., district attorney, Michael B. Nifong, violated so many legal and ethical rules that the case has become a national scandal. As many observers have concluded, Nifong's conduct portrayed a prosecutor gone amok, who manipulated a criminal complaint against Duke students as a weapon in his race for re-election, and exploited race and class divisions at the expense of justice and the truth. Although the case has been transferred to the state attorney general, Nifong's conduct should be examined because it illuminates the ethical guideposts for a prosecutor.

It was clear that Nifong faced a difficult prosecution. On the debit side, there was only the flimsiest evidence that the complainant had been raped, as she claimed: There was virtually no corroboration; her descriptions of the event and the perpetrators were riddled with inconsistencies; one of the alleged perpetrators had a powerful alibi; and there was no DNA evidence. But this was a case in which a prosecutor could pose as a "champion" of an oppressed racial minority against the socially privileged and elite. Nifong commenced a course of prosecutorial conduct that was demagogic and in bad faith.

In the weeks after the complaint was filed, Nifong gave dozens of inflammatory interviews to the media; they are now the subject of an ethics complaint against him by the Disciplinary Commission of the North Carolina State Bar. For example, Nifong repeated the complainant's allegations as factually accurate; asserted that "a rape did occur"; described the complainant's "struggle in order to be able to breathe"; characterized the defendants as "a bunch of hooligans"; accused Duke lacrosse players at the party of "stonewalling" his investigation; and suggested that scientific tests proved the complainant's allegations.

Moreover, Nifong arranged a photographic lineup that violated virtually every accepted guideline for lineups.

As she was shown the photographs, the victim's identification was bizarre. She identified one suspect as looking like one of the perpetrators, but "without the mustache." The person whom she identified never wore a mustache. She was shown other photos that included the defendants, and initially could not identify any of the pictures. Yet despite the weaknesses in her identification, the notorious dangers of eyewitness identifications, the capacity of lay juries to believe erroneous identifications as accurate and a prosecutor's duty to protect innocent people from fallible identification evidence, Nifong's position was clear, although misguided: "If she says, yes, it's them, I have an obligation to put that to the jury."

Finally, if there was any question that Nifong was pursuing this case unfairly and in violation of ethical and constitutional precepts, it was answered during the testimony of a forensic scientist, Dr. Brian W. Meehan, who tested the rape-kit swabs and underwear of the complainant for DNA. Meehan found traces of sperm and other DNA material from several men, but, most important, none of the DNA matched the defendants'. Although Meehan immediately communicated this finding to Nifong, Nifong directed Meehan not to include it in his report. When the court, after reviewing the report, asked Nifong: "So you represent that there are no other statements from Dr. Meehan?" he replied, "No other statements, no other statements made to me."

What are the ethics of criminal prosecution? Is a prosecutor the avenger of a person victimized by crime? Is he a neutral functionary who merely serves as a conduit between the complainant and the jury? Or does a prosecutor have as his principal role that of gatekeeper of the system of justice, to ensure that law enforcement behaves effectively, dispassionately and in the interests of arriving at the truth? To be sure, Nifong saw himself as an avenger and a functionary who could carelessly allow false and equivocal evidence to be presented to a fact-finder. Nifong did not assume the mantle of a gatekeeper to the system of justice.

Nifong's legacy contains an important message about the capacity of a prosecutor to exercise and abuse his enormous power. And while his conduct was so egregious as to border on aberrational, it is indeed worthwhile to review the prosecutor's function to ensure that Nifong is indeed history.

Gershman is a professor at Pace University School of Law and the author of Trial Error and Misconduct (Lexis Law Publishing 1997). Cohen is a partner at Strook & Strook & Lavan in New York, where he practices white-collar criminal law.

7

Judge Orders Trial for Ex-DA Charged in Embezzlement

A former district attorney was ordered Wednesday to stand trial on a charge he embezzled money his office had taken as evidence in a drug case, Attorney General Drew Edmondson said.

Associate District Judge David Martin of Cherokee County ended former prosecutor Richard Gray's preliminary hearing and ordered him to trial on one count of embezzlement, Edmondson said.

Gray was indicted in October by the state's multicounty grand jury on allegations of taking almost $9,000 in seized drug money while he was in office, Edmondson said.

The grand jury accused Gray of taking the drug money from the drug task force safe under the guise of putting the money into a safety deposit box, Edmondson said.

"We allege Gray took the money, but never deposited it with the county treasurer," Edmondson said. "We allege he is the last person to have possession of the funds."

Gray was former district attorney for Adair, Cherokee, Sequoyah and Wagoner counties. He was defeated in last year's election.

No trial date has been set, Edmondson said.

The multicounty grand jury previously indicted two others in the investigation into the Cherokee County district attorney's office, Edmondson's office said.

Janet Bickel, former assistant district attorney, and Vyrl Keeter, officer administrator, were indicted in January 2006 after the investigation discovered drug possession, tampering with evidence and a cover-up scheme, Edmondson's office said Wednesday.

Both pleaded guilty to the charges.

Bickel pleaded guilty in September to taking drugs from a Tahlequah crime scene for her own use and trying to cover it up. She also pleaded guilty to lying to a state grand jury about personal drug buys.

Keeter pleaded guilty to encouraging witnesses to lie in testimony before the state's multicounty grand jury.

"Our judicial system only works if those charged with executing it do so in a manner that upholds the public trust," Edmondson said. "A district attorney who violates that trust should be held to the same legal standard as the criminals they have themselves prosecuted."

Chapter 3

Sentencing and Corrections

Ethical Punishment and Treatment

1

Civil Commitment for Convicted Criminals

Donald A. Dripps

The US Supreme Court ruled in favor of a Kansas law allowing sexually violent predators to be committed as long as they had a mental abnormality in Kansas v. Hendricks. The ruling creates new standards for civil commitment, allowing people to be committed for being dangerous whether or not they have committed a crime or are mentally ill. The case involves pedophilia, an established mental illness. The court also disbursed with double jeopardy questions by stating this was a civil law and therefore did not constitute a criminal punishment.

The right-to-die decision may gamer more headlines, but the most troubling civil liberties decision of the term is Kansas v. Hendricks.(1) The case arose when Kansas authorities invoked the state's new sexually violent predator (SVP) law to commit Leroy Hendricks after he had served a sentence for child molestation.

Traditional civil commitment law requires a showing, by clear and convincing evidence, that the person to be committed is mentally ill and a danger to self or to others.(2) The SVP law also requires a showing of dangerousness but requires a different threshold finding than "mental illness."

The SVP statute applies only to people who have been charged with a sexual offense and convicted, found incompetent to stand trial, or acquitted on grounds of insanity or mental disease. And instead of requiring the state to show that the person is "mentally ill," the Kansas law requires the state to show that the person has a "mental abnormality."

The Kansas law threatens civil liberty in two general ways. First, as a substantive matter, the category of "mental abnormality" is a new and broader category than "mental illness." Officials are notoriously prone to overestimate dangerousness,(3) so the SVP law weakens the most important limit on civil commitment. For example, could a state define illegal drug use as a "mental abnormality" and thereby justify the commitment of any person who fails a urinalysis test for the drugs heroin, cocaine, or marijuana?

Second, procedurally, the act looks like an end run around the procedural safeguards of the criminal process. The state, subject to very broad Eighth Amendment limits, may punish criminal offenses as it pleases.(4)

There is little doubt that under current law a life sentence for a child molester with a record of similar offenses would survive constitutional scrutiny.

But the state of Kansas chose not to proceed criminally. Hendricks had served his time for the offense for which he was convicted. Then, in legislation not on the books at the time of Hendricks's crime, the state imposed the enormous new liability of indefinite commitment.

The U.S. Supreme Court unanimously rejected Hendricks's substantive challenge, but split 5 to 4 in upholding the procedural challenge based on the ex post facto law clause.

Substantive Due Process

The Supreme Court of Kansas ruled for Hendricks on the substantive ground.(5) Invoking substantive due process, the state high court held that civil commitment is constitutional only upon a showing of mental illness.

None of the nine justices of the U.S. Supreme Court agreed with this holding.(6) The unanimity suggests either that hard cases make bad law (Hendricks admitted an uncontrollable propensity to molest young children) or that the Kansas law is really no different than traditional civil commitment practice.

The latter interpretation is more comforting and finds some support in the language of the opinion. Justice Clarence Thomas wrote for the majority that contrary to Hendricks's assertion, the term "mental illness" is devoid of any talismanic significance. Not only do "psychiatrists disagree widely and frequently on what constitutes mental illness," but the Court itself has used a variety of expressions to describe the mental condition of those properly subject to civil confinement. Indeed we have never required state legislatures to adopt any particular nomenclature in drafting civil commitment statutes.... To the extent that the civil commitment statutes we have considered set forth criteria relating to an individual's inability to control his dangerousness, the Kansas act sets forth comparable criteria and Hendrick's condition doubtless satisfies those Criteria.(7)

The last point is crucial. Psychiatrists may classify pedophilia as a "personality disorder" rather than a mental illness, but the sense of the community is that a pedophile is less wicked than sick. Nobody would think of the greed inspiring robbery as a "mental abnormality." Nonetheless, the Court's reduction of the traditional two-step inquiry (mental illness and dangerousness) into a single inquiry into self control suggests a wide scope for civil commitment.

Every crime manifests a failure of self-control. Obvious examples include domestic violence and drug use. Why not lock up, indefinitely, members of competing gangs based on their propensity to attack their rivals?

The Hendricks case caused no dissent on this point because Hendricks seems very much like a sick, rather than an evil, person. Yet, in Foucha v. Louisiana, four members of the Court voted to uphold the civil commitment of an insanity-defense acquittee who was found to be no longer suffering from temporary psychosis but was diagnosed with an "antisocial personality."(8)

Justice Sandra Day O'Connor refused to uphold the commitment only because Foucha was confined in a penal institution rather than a treatment facility.(9) If an "antisocial personality" (which in lay language means having a mean streak) is enough to justify an inquiry into dangerousness, the Court could be prepared to accept commitment founded, for practical purposes, on dangerousness alone.

Such a development would be both oppressive and paradoxical. It would be oppressive because findings of dangerousness are easily made. If officials commit a person who would not have acted violently, nothing happens. If officials fail to commit a person who then commits serious crimes, political reaction will be intense. Given the problematic nature of predicting future behavior, and the applicable political incentives, arbitrary and discriminatory commitments would be the likely result.

Committing the sane but dangerous would be paradoxical as well as dangerous. The post-Hinckley return to the cognitive test of legal insanity was predicated on the assumption that people can control their behavior and are responsible when they fail to do so. Hendricks has now been held criminally responsible for behavior the state denies he can control.

It is by no means clear, however, that the Court would approve civil commitment of people whose lack of self-control is not attributable to some manifest mental aberration. The Court took pains to note that "mental health professionals who evaluated Hendricks diagnosed him as suffering from pedophilia, a condition the psychiatric profession itself classifies as a serious mental disorder." (10) That language looks in one direction, while the Foucha case looks in another.

Civil Punishment?

Once the substantive due process challenge was disposed of, the procedural issues became the focus of the case. Hendricks argued that the SVP commitment imposed additional punishment on him for an offense of which he was previously convicted, in violation of the ex post facto law clause and the double jeopardy clause. The majority rejected these contentions on the ground that the SVP law authorized civil, rather than criminal, proceedings.

Under traditional principles a person could be civilly committed upon a showing of mental illness and dangerousness independent of the criminal process. Civil commitment could take place even if the person had committed no crime, been convicted of a crime, or been acquitted of a crime. The procedures for commitment need not follow those required in criminal cases. For example, the Supreme Court has held that civil commitment orders need not be supported by proof beyond a reasonable doubt.(11)

Since civil commitment has nonpunitive purposes, the commitment following conviction violates neither the ex post facto law nor the double jeopardy clause. Where the dissenters parted company from the majority concerns the characterization of Hendricks's commitment as civil.

The dissenters emphasized the fact that commitment was triggered by a criminal offense and that the state courts had found a punitive purpose.(12) The majority emphasized the state's characterization of the proceedings as civil and the representation by the state's counsel at argument that extensive treatment was now being provided to people committed under the SVP law.(13)

Reasonable judges are likely to disagree about where the civil/criminal line should be drawn in particular cases. The more fundamental question is the substantive one of whether sane but dangerous people can be confined solely to protect society. A case like Hendricks does not quite squarely raise this issue, because Hendricks had in fact committed an offense for which he could be detained for a very long period.

If Kansas law provided that sexually violent predators who are convicted of rape or child molestation be sentenced to life in prison, subject to release upon a finding that they are no longer dangerous, no serious constitutional question would arise. At least with respect to cases that arise after its adoption, all the sexually violent predator law does is to change the sentence applicable to sexual crimes. What the state can do directly it should be allowed to do indirectly.

Even the Foucha case did not quite raise this issue, for Foucha had been acquitted on the criminal charge on the ground of insanity, not on the ground of, say, mistaken identity or self-defense. Arguably the state can, so far as the Constitution is concerned, dispense with the insanity defense completely. Again arguably, the Louisiana scheme simply imposed a condition on invocation of the insanity defense.

Nonetheless, Hendricks is cause for concern. It joins a growing line of modem cases in which the Court has accepted confining people in institutions absent a criminal conviction.(14) To all appearances, the Court is sliding down a slippery slope, one that ends in state power to confine people who are not insane and who have committed no crime.

Notes

1. No. 95-1649, 1997 WL 338555 (U.S. June 23, 1997). Subsequent page references to the opinion are to the WESTLAW pagination.

2. See Addington v. Texas, 441 U.S. 418 (1979).

3. See, eg., JOHN MONAHAN, THE CLINICAL PREDICTION OF VIOLENT BEHAVIOR (1981).

4. See, e.g., Harmelin v. Michigan, 501 U.S. 957 (1991).

5. In re Hendricks, 912 P.2d 129 (Kan. 1996).

6. See Hendricks, 1997 WL 338555, at *6; id. at *15 (Kennedy, J., concurring); id. at *16 (Breyer, J., dissenting). Breyer's opinion was joined by Justices Ginsburg, Souter, and Stevens, but Ginsburg declined to join this section of the Breyer dissent; she did, however, write separately to explain her views.

7. Id. at *8 (citations omitted) (emphasis added).

8. 504 U.S. 71 (1992).

9. Id. at 86 (O'Connor, J., concurring).

10. Hendricks, 1997 WL 338555, at *8. Breyer was even more concerned about limiting civil commitment to cases of mental disturbance. See id. at *17-18.

11. Addington, 441 U.S. 418, 431.

12. Hendricks, 1997 WL 338555, at *21-22.

13. Id. at *9-11, *13.

14. See Reno v. Flores, 507 U.S. 292 (1993); United States v. Salerno, 481 U.S. 739 (1987); Schall v. Martin, 467 U.S. 253 (1984).

Donald A. Dripps is a professor at the University of Illinois College of Law.

2

Another chance?

Counting Petty Crime in 'Three-Strikes' Law Wrong, Critics Say

Susan Herendeen

Mike Salerno had $300 in his pocket, more than enough to pay for the $64.99 Dale Earnhardt Jr. jacket he is accused of stealing.

He insists a clerk at Kmart removed the NASCAR jacket from a lost-and-found box and gave it to him because he was cold.

A Ceres police report tells a different story, suggesting that Salerno faced a moral dilemma as he browsed the store six months ago, because he paid for shoes he seemed ready to steal, but waltzed out the door with a jacket he didn't buy.

If either version of events results in a felony conviction, Salerno could be sentenced to 25 years to life in prison under California's "three strikes" law.

Salerno, 41, of Modesto, insists he is innocent.

"I went there to shop," he said. "Not shoplift."

Salerno could join more than 7,800 inmates who have received their third strike under the nation's toughest sentencing law, including more than 100 people from Stanislaus County.

About 56 percent of third-strikers in California's prisons, including 70 percent of the third-strikers from Stanislaus County, received their third strike for nonviolent crimes, such as theft or drug possession.

The law has a controversial history. Critics contend that a third strike for a petty crime amounts to unconstitutional cruel and unusual punishment.

The U.S. Supreme Court upheld the law in 2003, saying states have a right to isolate repeat offenders from society to protect public safety.

Voters rejected an effort to amend the law a year later, but the debate is not over. Two Southern California prosecutors are trying to get two initiatives before voters this fall. The initiatives would give shorter sen-tences to third-strikers whose third conviction is for a petty crime.

Warehousing Inmates

In Stanislaus County, prosecutors say they are comfortable with the law as written. Chief Deputy District Attorney John Goold said his office usually charges two-strikers who are suspected in new crimes with a felony, although they may resolve a case for less.

He said some people simply are hard-wired for crime.

"If someone has strike priors and they've been in and out of jail for 15 of 18 years since they were adults, those people are doing nothing but continually committing crimes and preying on other people," Goold said. "They deserve to be warehoused, in our opinion, and that's what the 'three strikes' law allows."

Salerno has a long history of legal trouble, including two strikes stemming from a drug-crazed assault on his neighbors 10 years ago.

In the Kmart case, prosecutors charged him with second-degree burglary -- rather than petty theft, the standard charge for shoplifting -- because of his criminal history.

Salerno has been in custody since his Feb. 8 arrest, held on $250,000 bail.

As he awaits trial, Salerno is both defiant and eager to prove that he deserves another chance.

Interviewed at the Public Safety Center, Salerno said he reads the Bible every day. He said he has given his life over to God and proudly talked about his recent jailhouse baptism.

He said he has been framed by people prejudiced against parolees and believes police raised the charges against him as soon as they realized he had a criminal record.

"I'm in here for a coat I didn't steal," Salerno said.

If he is convicted, a prosecutor could ask a judge to void one of Salerno's prior strikes. He received one reprieve already as part of a plea bargain in 2000, when he pleaded guilty to drug sales.

Or a judge could hand down a third strike. A sentence of 25 years to life results in a minimum of 20 years behind bars.

Defense attorney Martin Baker said he thinks Salerno has a good shot at a reprieve, in part because prosecutors must prove he went to Kmart intending to steal, a key element of a burglary charge.

"He certainly had more than enough money to pay," Baker said. "It looks to me like some kind of misunderstanding or absentmindedness on the part of the staff at Kmart or even Mr. Salerno himself."

Myles Kuikahi, a bail bondsman who befriended Salerno, thinks it's ridiculous to warehouse a shoplifter for the rest of his life.

"C'mon, it's a jacket," he said. "Let us go pay for it."

Salerno is to return to Stanislaus County Superior Court on Aug. 9, when a judge is ex-pected to set a trial date.

Goold said he believes the law keeps repeat offenders off the streets.

"The person who is being punished under the 'three strikes' law is getting a life sentence because they repeatedly commit crimes," he said.

Years Behind Bars

According to the California Department of Corrections, prison cost $34,150 a year per inmate in 2005-06.

Salerno has spent 26 years behind bars, in juvenile hall, jail and prison. Court records include police reports and psychological evaluations that repeat his claims.

He said he started smoking marijuana at 8 and was taken away from alcoholic parents at 9. He claims to have been sexually abused in a foster home. He said his two brothers committed suicide.

He has been convicted of breaking into an auto parts store, receiving drugs through the mail, possessing drugs and selling drugs, according to court records in Tacoma, Wash., and Modesto.

He committed his most serious crime, the one that earned him two strikes, in 1996. He took too many pills prescribed by a psychiatrist, grabbed two butcher knives and lunged at two neighbors who court records said caught him trying to illegally tap into a cable TV line.

The altercation ended with Salerno begging Modesto police officers to shoot him. He got four years in prison instead.

He was homeless and out of money, having spent the $200 he received upon his release from Deuel Vocational Institution near Tracy on a bus ticket to Modesto, a motel room, pants and a pair of sneakers.

He was mad at a parole officer who wouldn't give him more food vouchers and angry with the Social Security Administration because he applied for disability but hadn't received any payments.

He found himself back at Deuel for three months in spring 2004 on a parole hold because he failed his required drug tests. Later, he completed drug treatment.

Wife, Minister Pray for Him

Things started looking up when Salerno moved in with a neighbor who attends church regularly and won't put up with drugs.

Mike and Monica Salerno married a few months later, on Valentine's Day in 2005, and moved into a rented mobile home.

He tagged along to some of her classes at Modesto Junior College and found a few odd jobs.

The couple survived on disability payments from Social Security: $836 a month for him and $726 a month for her, according to Monica Salerno. He qualifies for aid because of mental health issues, and she has back spasms that keep her from holding a steady job, they said.

Salerno said he went to Kmart on Feb. 8 to buy his wife an anniversary gift. He never came home.

Monica Salerno said she believes her husband will be free again. "I don't think he was stealing or shoplifting," she said.

Pastor Greg Young, leader of The Healing House ministry in Modesto, said he believes Salerno's newfound faith is real.

He visits Salerno regularly, and says Salerno needs to make peace with himself, whether or not he gets out of jail.

"I don't think he would have come face to face with having to make some real serious changes in his life if this situation hadn't arisen," Young said.

3

Prisons Rife With Physical Abuse

Guards Struck Inmates, Stood Idle During Beatings

Holly Becka and Doug J. Swanson

Eighteen-year-old Erik Rodriguez was fighting off an assault from another inmate at the state juvenile prison in Corsicana when three other boys rushed into his dorm room.

They held his arms and legs, he said, while one of the inmates "kicked me on the side of my jaw about 20 times." When they finished, he said, "blood poured out of my face like a fountain."

While Mr. Rodriguez absorbed the blows, the two guards for his dorm at the Corsicana Residential Treatment Center were elsewhere. They later were fired for neglect.

The teen's mother said that the Texas Youth Commission assured her that its high-security facility for juveniles with mental or emotional problems would provide her son the best care it had to offer. "I was told that all the boys would be supervised 24-7," Alice Smith said. "As long as they did what they're supposed to do, they would be safe."

What happened at Corsicana is not an isolated incident. Texas Rangers, who were dispatched across the state this week to investigate sexual misconduct at TYC prisons, will also learn of widespread physical abuse.

Records obtained by The Dallas Morning News under the Texas Public Information Act include accounts of guards striking handcuffed inmates, encouraging inmates to fight one another and standing idle while beatings occurred. In one case, a guard threatened to throw a handcuffed inmate off a roof.

"Every day that the ... investigation moves forward, it shines more light on the numerous failures throughout the TYC system," said Ted Royer, spokesman for Gov. Rick Perry. "We suspect there are vast numbers of cases of potential criminal activity that have not been reported and that no one has been accountable for."

TYC substantiated 165 allegations of abuse in 2005 and 105 last year. The agency was unable to provide The News on Thursday a breakdown of those numbers by unit or type of abuse alleged.

An agency spokesman later referred questions to the governor's office. But the governor's spokesman said all "technical information" had to come from TYC.

Frequent Abuse

In Corsicana alone, previously released TYC records show, physical abuse was frequent.

In 2000, for example, a guard was fired after a young man alleged the guard "restrained him for no reason and has been letting students punch, kick, hit him, spit on him and urinate on his bed."

Another Corsicana guard kept his job but received probation in 2003 after a staffer saw him "place his hand on a youth's throat and hold him against the wall. ... When [the guard] released the youth, he appeared to drop down to the floor as if he had been lifted in the air by a few inches."

A month later, a guard at the Corsicana prison was accused of slamming a young man's head on the floor several times and stomping "the student on the left side of his head." The guard was fired.

Similar problems have surfaced in many other TYC prisons, which house about 4,000 of the state's most violent and incorrigible offenders, ages 10 to 21.

Last year at the Ron Jackson Unit in Brownwood, TYC investigators substantiated an allegation that "staff placed his hands around the youth's throat while the youth was in parade rest, and slammed him twice against the concrete wall."

And at the West Texas State School in Pyote -- where allegations of a sexual abuse cover-up brought down the agency's head and board chairman -- TYC investigators filed this account of a 2005 incident when two inmates climbed onto a dorm roof:

"The youths DD and AS ... were handcuffed by JCO [juvenile correctional officer], who then began kicking DD in the side. JCO approached AS, stepped on him, kicked him three times, and pulled him up to a standing position.

"JCO then took AS to the edge of the roof and threatened to throw him off."

The officer was given 90 days' probation.

Will Harrell, executive director of the American Civil Liberties Union of Texas, says that of the records he keeps on physical abuse among youth inmates, the Crockett, Giddings and Evins juvenile units are by far the worst.

The Evins prison is under investigation by the U.S. Justice Department for TYC's handling of an inmate riot and its aftermath in 2004.

Mr. Harrell said the problem of inmate abuse is systemic.

"The guards are overwhelmed," he said. "They have one [guard] to every 25 kids in a dormitory setting. ...These problems, what you see in West Texas and all these facilities -- physical and sexual abuse -- are a predictable outcome of this flawed system."

Inadequate Supervision

Overwhelmed or inattentive guards were found to be a major factor in the Corsicana beating of Mr. Rodriguez in October 2006.

A tall, thin young man with a buzz cut, Mr. Rodriguez admits he has a history of problems at TYC. He has been disciplined repeatedly for arguments with -- and, in at least one case, an assault on -- staff members.

He was sent to TYC because he broke into three homes in San Antonio. He has been found to have Tourette's syndrome and obsessive compulsive disorder, and he receives medications for those. He is still trying to earn his GED.

Mr. Rodriguez said that just before the October assault, he got into a mild dispute, over cutting in line, with another inmate in the cafeteria.

After lunch, in Cottage 15, the same inmate approached him in the restroom. "He said, 'We need to talk in the room man-to-man,' " Mr. Rodriguez recalled.

They went to Mr. Rodriguez's bedroom. The other youth said the cafeteria confrontation had caused him to lose face. "He says, 'You need to stop saying that stuff. You make me look bad,' " Mr. Rodriguez said.

Then the inmate began hitting him, he said. "We're in the room fighting for about 30 seconds. He hits me in the groin. ... Then three other people come in."

"They just took turns" beating him, he said.

Mr. Rodriguez said he staggered to the bathroom and washed himself. About two hours later, he was taken to a Corsicana hospital emergency room. "My face was so swollen, it looked like it had been stung by 20 bees."

Ray Worsham, director of TYC's Office of Youth Care Investigations, said guards didn't adequately monitor the young inmates.

"They slipped over to the control panel -- it's not concealed or in a separate room or anything -- but somehow they managed to buzz that [dorm room] door," Mr. Worsham said. "Those two staff were not doing their duty essentially."

Confidential TYC investigative records obtained by The News say it's unclear who opened the door.

Mr. Rodriguez thinks the guards purposely let him be assaulted because they don't like him. He and his mother said they will file a federal lawsuit against TYC next week alleging that.

His lawyer, civil rights attorney James W. Myart Jr. of San Antonio, said the case was indicative of widespread abuse in TYC.

"It's pretty egregious what happened, because it was actually staff members who perpetrated it, set it up, opened the cage doors and let it happen," he said.

Mr. Rodriguez's mother, an employee of KENS-TV in San Antonio -- owned by Belo Corp., The News' parent company -- said she is extremely upset about her son.

"I'm very worried on a daily basis," Ms. Smith said. "I just worry about him making it through the night."

"They expect the boys to follow rules but, on the other hand, the staff are not," she added.

Repeat Problems

Agency records obtained by The News show that one of the two guards fired in Mr. Rodriguez's incident was well known to TYC investigators.

Investigators confirmed at least seven allegations of mistreatment against Greg Ardister from 2000 to 2006, according to a review by The News. They were unable to confirm several other allegations against him.

Mr. Ardister could not be located for comment.

Mr. Worsham acknowledged that the former corrections officer had a "high number" of various types of alleged mistreatment.

"If you were to take all of our employees, he would be in the higher group" for allegations, he said.

In March 2001, for example, staffers searching inmates' rooms found photos of Mr. Ardister posing with several youths who were flashing gang signs and wearing Mr. Ardister's TYC jacket, according to agency records.

"Mr. Ardister actually took pictures with the students and allowed them to be gang affiliated in the pictures," the records say.

Mr. Worsham said TYC guards don't have specific uniforms, but they do buy jackets to promote morale and show the unit where they work.

"I suppose they thought they were having some lighthearted fun, but ... it was bad sense on his part to participate in gang sign-throwing activity," he said.

Also in March 2001, a youth alleged he was being physically abused by other inmates, and that staffers, including Mr. Ardister, were "doing nothing about it."

Following the investigations, Mr. Ardister was put on probation for the two incidents, records show.

A few years later, in June, July and August of 2003, TYC investigators looked into three separate allegations that Mr. Ardister was having inappropriate relationships with juvenile inmates. The allegations against him ranged from inappropriate touching to an accusation that a female inmate had kissed Mr. Ardister. Each of the allegations was confirmed, and Mr. Ardister was placed on probation, TYC records show.

In June 2006, investigators again looked into Mr. Ardister's behavior. Authorities confirmed that he used excessive force while restraining a boy, according to TYC's records. The young man was left with facial abrasions and a cut lip.

At the time, Mr. Ardister also was under investigation for an allegation that he and three other TYC staffers put a naked youth into a feces-filled room marked with an "out of order" sign on the door, records show.

Attorney Myart was outraged to learn from a reporter that Mr. Ardister had a history of problems at Corsicana.

"The fact that they fired these individuals is of absolutely no consequence because the top officials had or should have had the entire record of these employees, which in at least one case, clearly indicates they had direct knowledge of his misconduct prior to what happened to my client," he said.

Understaffed Unit

The other guard fired after the Rodriguez beating, Sharon Hodge, said in an interview that she is fighting her termination. She said that the unit was understaffed at the time and that the incident was not her fault.

"I didn't do anything [wrong], and I feel like they fired me for no reason because we were understaffed," she said. "I don't know anything about it because I was not working that side [of the dorm]. I got involved because I was working that day.

"I'm saying it was the other person's fault," Ms. Hodge said. "I just want my name cleared."

The confidential investigative records obtained by The News say Ms. Hodge told authorities that inmates distracted the staff, especially Mr. Ardister, with magazines "with girls in bikinis and underwear."

Video evidence shows there were enough staff distractions to allow youths to move unsupervised down a hallway, the records say.

"Video surveillance does not provide conclusive evidence as to who may have unlocked room #6," the investigative report states. "All other details of the incident time period are different. Neither JCO Hodge nor JCO Ardister have any explanation for the incident. Instead, they blame each other for the lack of supervision. This demonstrates knowledge that both were aware of dorm issues, but neither was willing to do anything about it."

Staff writer Emily Ramshaw in Austin contributed to this report.

4

Idaho Prisoners Abused at Private Texas Prison

Inmate Says He Was Handcuffed, Beaten and Maced; Correctional Officers Have Been Disciplined

Shawna Gamache

Correctional officers at a private Texas prison have been disciplined for abusing Idaho prisoners this spring, the state Correction Department said Thursday.

At least half a dozen department employees, including department Director Tom Beauclair, flew to Texas after the department received complaints from inmates and family members, department spokeswoman Melinda Keckler said in response to an inquiry from the Idaho Statesman about allegations of abuse.

The state team inspected the Newton County Correctional Center in Newton, operated by Geo Group Inc. The company disciplined security staff members in response to the team's findings, Keckler said.

"We have received concerns from several parties, all in relation to one or two specific incidents in the Texas facility," Keckler said. "(Department) employees interviewed offenders and staff and observed the physical operations of the facility, and as a result of that, some corrective action was taken on some employees in Texas."

Keckler said she could not describe the nature of the abuse or specify how prison employees were disciplined. The media contact for the Geo Group was on vacation and could not be reached, and the prison's warden would not comment.

Keckler said the department is satisfied that the Newton prison is complying with its agreement with Idaho.

The state has turned to out-of-state prisons to handle inmate overflow from Idaho's jam-packed prisons. In mid-March, 150 prisoners were moved to the Texas prison. Since then, 270 more Idaho prisoners have been transferred from the Prairie Correctional Facility in Appleton, Minn. after that private prison needed to make space for more Minnesota prisoners. All out-of-state Idaho prisoners are now housed at the 872-bed Newton prison, as are prisoners from Arizona and Texas and federal immigrations and customs detainees.

Josie Daniel, a 32-year-old homemaker from Fruitland, said her brother, Eddie Daniel, an Idaho inmate transferred to Texas in April, was interviewed by Correction Department employees in response to abuses he and six other prisoners suffered in early April.

In a letter Josie Daniel received from her brother April 14, he said he and six other prisoners had been put in an isolation area without explanation for five days from April 3 to April 7. On the fifth day they were handcuffed, beaten and maced by 15 people, the letter claimed.

"So these people came in ... and take turns beating us up," Daniel wrote. "And when I say beating us I mean beating us, kicking us in the face ... They went cell to cell during this."

According to the letter, the beatings of the prisoners stopped when the warden intervened.

Eddie Daniel also said food, showers and recreation time were withheld, and beatings continued after the first incident.

"Even though we're in Texas, Idaho is still responsible for us," he wrote. "You need to call IDOC and let them know what's going on. Now every day they come to our cells threatening to beat us again."

Josie Daniel said she contacted at least five IDOC employees, including Keckler, to report the abuse.

Eddie Daniel is serving a six-year sentence for drug trafficking and had already served six months of it in Idaho, according to Josie Daniel, who served a two-year sentence herself for grand theft that she committed when she was 19. Josie Daniel said her brother had served five years in Idaho prisons for earlier crimes and never complained of mistreatment or abuse.

"My brother is the kind of person that he has a lot of pride, and he's not going to ask anyone for help," Josie Daniel said. "My heart sunk when I read this letter because he is pleading for help."

Keckler said the department had not received any abuse complaints at the private Minnesota facility. Idaho staffers will continue with routine checks of the Texas prison and will investigate any future complaints, she said.

"Of course whenever we have charges of abuse we take them very seriously," Keckler said.

Chapter 4

Government Policies

When Ethics Collide with National Security

1

FBI Surveillance Capability More Extensive Than Once Thought

Documents obtained by the Electronic Frontier Foundation have provided disturbing details about the extent of the FBI's ability to monitor the communications of American citizens. According to Wired News reporter Ryan Singel, "The FBI has quietly built a sophisticated, point-and-click surveillance system that performs instant wiretaps on almost any communications device, according to nearly a thousand pages of restricted documents newly released under the Freedom of information Act."

Known as "DCSNet," for Digital Collection System Network, it closely connects FBI wiretapping installations with the nation's telecommunications infrastructure. According to Wired, "It is far more intricately woven into the nation's telecom infrastructure than observers suspected. It's a 'comprehensive wiretap system that intercepts wire-line phones, cellular phones, SMS and push-to-talk systems,' says Steven Bellovin, a Columbia University computer science professor and longtime surveillance expert."

According to the Wired report, the FBI's private network is run by telecommunications company Sprint Nextel. How powerful is this surveillance network? According to Wired: "The network allows an FBI agent in New York, for example, to remotely set up a wiretap on a cell phone based in Sacramento, California, and immediately learn the phone's location, then begin receiving conversations, text messages and voicemail pass codes in New York. With a few keystrokes, the agent can route the recordings to language specialists for translation."

2

Military Expands Intelligence Role in U.S.

Eric Lichtblau; Mark Mazzetti

The Pentagon has been using a little-known power to obtain banking and credit records of hundreds of Americans and others suspected of terrorism or espionage inside the United States, part of an aggressive expansion by the military into domestic intelligence gathering.

The C.I.A. has also been issuing what are known as national security letters to gain access to financial records from American companies, though it has done so only rarely, intelligence officials say.

Banks, credit card companies and other financial institutions receiving the letters usually have turned over documents voluntarily, allowing investigators to examine the financial assets and transactions of American military personnel and civilians, officials say.

The F.B.I., the lead agency on domestic counterterrorism and espionage, has issued thousands of national security letters since the attacks of Sept. 11, 2001, provoking criticism and court challenges from civil liberties advocates who see them as unjustified intrusions into Americans' private lives.

But it was not previously known, even to some senior counterterrorism officials, that the Pentagon and the Central Intelligence Agency have been using their own "noncompulsory" versions of the letters. Congress has rejected several attempts by the two agencies since 2001 for authority to issue mandatory letters, in part because of concerns about the dangers of expanding their role in domestic spying.

The military and the C.I.A. have long been restricted in their domestic intelligence operations, and both are barred from conducting traditional domestic law enforcement work. The C.I.A.'s role within the United States has been largely limited to recruiting people to spy on foreign countries.

Carl Kropf, a spokesman for the director of national intelligence, said intelligence agencies like the C.I.A. used the letters on only a ''limited basis.''

Pentagon officials defended the letters as valuable tools and said they were part of a broader strategy since the Sept. 11 attacks to use more aggressive intelligence-gathering tactics -- a priority of former Defense Secretary Donald H. Rumsfeld. The letters ''provide tremendous leads to follow and often with which to corroborate other evidence in the context of counterespionage and counterterrorism,'' said Maj. Patrick Ryder, a Pentagon spokesman.

Government lawyers say the legal authority for the Pentagon and the C.I.A. to use national security letters in gathering domestic records dates back nearly three decades and, by their reading, was strengthened by the antiterrorism law known as the USA Patriot Act.

Pentagon officials said they used the letters to follow up on a variety of intelligence tips or leads. While they would not provide details about specific cases, military intelligence officials with knowledge of them said the military had issued the letters to collect financial records regarding a government contractor with unexplained wealth, for example, and a chaplain at Guantanamo Bay erroneously suspected of aiding prisoners at the facility.

Usually, the financial documents collected through the letters do not establish any links to espionage or terrorism and have seldom led to criminal charges, military officials say. Instead, the letters often help eliminate suspects.

''We may find out this person has unexplained wealth for reasons that have nothing to do with being a spy, in which case we're out of it,'' said Thomas A. Gandy, a senior Army counterintelligence official.

But even when the initial suspicions are unproven, the documents have intelligence value, military officials say. In the next year, they plan to incorporate the records into a database at the Counterintelligence Field Activity office at the Pentagon to track possible threats against the military, Pentagon officials said. Like others interviewed, they would speak only on the condition of anonymity.

Military intelligence officers have sent letters in up to 500 investigations over the last five years, two officials estimated. The number of letters is likely to be well into the thousands, the officials said, because a single case often generates letters to multiple financial institutions. For its part, the C.I.A. issues a handful of national security letters each year, agency officials said. Congressional officials said members of the House and Senate

Intelligence Committees had been briefed on the use of the letters by the military and the C.I.A.

Some national security experts and civil liberties advocates are troubled by the C.I.A. and military taking on domestic intelligence activities, particularly in light of recent disclosures that the Counterintelligence Field Activity office had maintained files on Iraq war protesters in the United States in violation of the military's own guidelines. Some experts say the Pentagon has adopted an overly expansive view of its domestic role under the guise of ''force protection,'' or efforts to guard military installations.

''There's a strong tradition of not using our military for domestic law enforcement,'' said Elizabeth Rindskopf Parker, a former general counsel at both the National Security Agency and the C.I.A. who is the dean at the McGeorge School of Law at the University of the Pacific. ''They're moving into territory where historically they have not been authorized or presumed to be operating.''

Similarly, John Radsan, an assistant general counsel at the C.I.A. from 2002 to 2004 and now a law professor at William Mitchell College of Law in St. Paul, said, ''The C.I.A. is not supposed to have any law enforcement powers, or internal security functions, so if they've been issuing their own national security letters, they better be able to explain how they don't cross the line.''

The Pentagon's expanded intelligence-gathering role, in particular, has created occasional conflicts with other federal agencies. Pentagon efforts to post American military officers at embassies overseas to gather intelligence for counterterrorism operations or future war plans has rankled some State Department and C.I.A. officials, who see the military teams as duplicating and potentially interfering with the intelligence agency.

In the United States, the Federal Bureau of Investigation has complained about military officials dealing directly with local police -- rather than through the bureau -- for assistance in responding to possible terrorist threats against a military base. F.B.I. officials say the threats have often turned out to be uncorroborated and, at times, have stirred needless anxiety.

The military's frequent use of national security letters has sometimes caused concerns from the businesses receiving them, a counterterrorism official said. Lawyers at financial institutions, which routinely provide records to the F.B.I. in law enforcement investigations, have contacted bureau officials to say they were confused by the scope of the military's requests and whether they were obligated to turn the records over, the official said.

Companies are not eager to turn over sensitive financial data about customers to the government, the official said, ''so the more this is done, and the more poorly it's done, the more pushback there is for the F.B.I.''

The bureau has frequently relied on the letters in recent years to gather telephone and Internet logs, financial information and other records in terrorism investigations, serving more than 9,000 letters in 2005, according to a Justice Department tally. As an investigative tool, the letters present relatively few hurdles; they can be authorized by supervisors rather than a court. Passage of the Patriot Act in October 2001 lowered the standard for issuing the letters, requiring only that the documents sought be ''relevant'' to an investigation and allowing records requests for more peripheral figures, not just targets of an inquiry.

Some Democrats have accused the F.B.I. of using the letters for fishing expeditions, and the American Civil Liberties Union won court challenges in two cases, one for library records in Connecticut and the other for Internet records in Manhattan. Concerned about possible abuses, Congress imposed new safeguards in extending the Patriot Act last year, in part by making clear that recipients of national security letters could contact a lawyer and seek court review. Congress also directed the Justice Department inspector general to study the F.B.I.'s use of the letters, a review that is continuing.

Unlike the F.B.I., the military and the C.I.A. do not have wide-ranging authority to seek records on Americans in intelligence investigations. But the expanded use of national security letters has allowed the Pentagon and the intelligence agency to collect records on their own. Sometimes, military or C.I.A. officials work with the F.B.I. to seek records, as occurred with an American translator who had worked for the military in Iraq and was suspected of having ties to insurgents.

After the Sept. 11 attacks, Mr. Rumsfeld directed military lawyers and intelligence officials to examine their legal authorities to collect intelligence both inside the United States and abroad. They concluded that the Pentagon had ''way more'' legal tools than it had been using, a senior Defense Department official said.

Military officials say the Right to Financial Privacy Act of 1978, which establishes procedures for government access to sensitive banking data, first authorized them to issue national security letters. The military had used the letters sporadically for years, officials say, but the pace accelerated in late 2001, when lawyers and intelligence officials concluded that the Patriot Act strengthened their ability to use the letters to seek financial records on a voluntary basis and to issue mandatory letters to obtain credit ratings, the officials said.

The Patriot Act does not specifically mention military intelligence or C.I.A. officials in connection with the national security letters.

Some F.B.I. officials said they were surprised by the Pentagon's interpretation of the law when military officials first informed them of it. ''It was a very broad reading of the law,'' a former counterterrorism official said.

While the letters typically have been used to trace the financial transactions of military personnel, they also have been used to investigate civilian contractors and people with no military ties who may pose a threat to the military, officials said. Military officials say they regard the letters as one of the least intrusive means to gather evidence. When a full investigation is opened, one official said, it has now become ''standard practice'' to issue such letters.

One prominent case in which letters were used to obtain financial records, according to two military officials, was that of a Muslim chaplain at Guantanamo Bay, Cuba, who was suspected in 2003 of aiding terror suspects imprisoned at the facility. The espionage case against the chaplain, James J. Yee, soon collapsed.

Eugene Fidell, a defense lawyer for the former chaplain and a military law expert, said he was unaware that military investigators may have used national security letters to obtain financial information about Mr. Yee, nor was he aware that the military had ever claimed the authority to issue the letters.

Mr. Fidell said he found the practice ''disturbing,'' in part because the military does not have the same checks and balances when it comes to Americans' civil rights as does the F.B.I. ''Where is the accountability?'' he asked. ''That's the evil of it -- it doesn't leave fingerprints.''

Even when a case is closed, military officials said they generally maintain the records for years because they may be relevant to future intelligence inquiries. Officials at the Pentagon's counterintelligence unit say they plan to incorporate those records into a database, called Portico, on intelligence leads. The financial documents will not be widely disseminated, but limited to investigators, an intelligence official said.

''You don't want to destroy something only to find out that the same guy comes up in another report and you don't know that he was investigated before,'' the official said.

The Counterintelligence Field Activity office, created in 2002 to better coordinate the military's efforts to combat foreign intelligence services, has drawn criticism for some domestic intelligence activities.

The agency houses an antiterrorist database of intelligence tips and threat reports, known as Talon, which had been collecting information on antiwar planning meetings at churches, libraries and other locations. The Defense Department has since tightened its procedures for what kind of information is allowed into the Talon database, and the counterintelligence office also purged more than 250 incident reports from the database that officials determined should never have been included because they centered on lawful political protests by people opposed to the war in Iraq.

3

Roundup of Aliens After 9/11 Ruled 'Crude' But Lawful

Tom Perrotta

Federal authorities responding to the Sept. 11, 2001, terrorist attacks did not violate the law by arresting aliens of Middle Eastern descent for immigration violations and holding them for long periods as they investigated possible ties to terrorism, a federal judge ruled yesterday.

Eastern District Judge John Gleeson, ruling on a motion to dismiss in a 99-page decision, said the government's approach might have been "crude" but was not illegal.

"After the September 11 attacks, our government used all available law enforcement tools to ferret out the persons responsible for those atrocities and to prevent additional acts of terrorism," he wrote in Turkmen v. Ashcroft , 02 CV 2307. "We should expect nothing less."

However, the judge declined to dismiss abuse claims by eight illegal aliens who had sued as part of a class action lawsuit over their detentions at the Metropolitan Detention Center (MDC) in Brooklyn and the Passaic County Jail in New Jersey.

Their allegations of abuse-- including sleep deprivation, physical beatings, strip searches and a failure to allow them to speak to attorneys--have been bolstered by extensive findings from the Office of the Inspector General (NYLJ, Dec. 24, 2003).

The men, who were held between three and seven months before being cleared of terrorism ties, have since been deported or have agreed to leave the country. Seven of them are Muslims; one is Hindu.

Among the defendants named in the suit are former Attorney General John Ashcroft; FBI Director Robert Mueller; James

A. Ziglar, the former Commissioner of the Immigration and Naturalization Service; and numerous wardens at the MDC.

Judge Gleeson said his decision had noting to do with the "extraordinary circumstances" of Sept. 11. Instead, he said, his reasoning was rooted in immigration law.

"Such national emergencies are not cause to relax the rights guaranteed in our Constitution," Judge Gleeson wrote. "Yet regarding immigration matters such as this, the Constitution assigns to the political branches all but the most minimal authority in making the delicate balancing judgments that attend all difficult constitutional questions."

In particular, the judge cited Reno v. American-Arab Anti-Discrimination Comm. ("AADC") , 525 U.S. 471 (1999) and Zadvydas v. Davis , 533 U.S. 678 (2001).

In, AADC , the U.S. Supreme Court ruling interpreted the Illegal Immigration Reform and Immigrant Responsibility Act. The Court held that the act deprived courts of jurisdiction over a suit in which resident aliens claimed they had been unconstitutionally targeted for deportation because of their affiliation with a politically unpopular group.

In Zadvydas , the Court held that the Immigration and Nationality Act's post-removal-period had a presumptive limit of six months. If an illegal alien then provided a reason to believe that removal was not likely in the foreseeable future, the government could further detain him or her only on a showing of evidence.

Judge Gleeson also cited U.S. v. Scopo , 19 F.3d 777, a 1994 ruling from the U.S. Court of Appeals for the Second Circuit that affirmed a police officer's right to pull over a car for a traffic violation if he wanted to search a suspect's car for a handgun.

"In the immediate aftermath of these events, when the government had only the barest of information about the hijackers to aid its efforts to prevent further terrorist attacks, it determined to subject to greater scrutiny aliens who shared characteristics with the hijackers, such as violating their visas and national origin and/or religion," the judge wrote. "As a tool fashioned by the executive branch to ferret out information to prevent additional terrorist attacks, this approach may have been crude, but it was not so irrational or outrageous as to warrant judicial intrusion into an area in which courts have little experience and less expertise."

'Profoundly Disturbing'

The Center for Constitutional Rights, which represented the plaintiffs, attacked the judge's decision and said it would appeal.

"This ruling gives a green light to racial profiling and prolonged detention of non-citizens at the whim of the president," said Rachel Meeropol, an attorney at the center who is litigating the case. "The decision is profoundly disturbing because it legitimizes the fact that the Bush administration rounded up and imprisoned our clients because of their religion and race."

Charles Miller, a spokesman for the Department of Justice's Civil Division, said: "The department is very pleased that the court upheld the decision to detain plaintiffs, all of whom were illegal aliens, until national security investigations were completed and plaintiffs were removed from the country. As for the court's decisions on the conditions of confinement in the detention facilities, the department is still reviewing the court's opinion and considering whether or not to appeal it."

Michael Winger, a special counsel at Covington & Burling, which is representing the plaintiffs pro bono, said Judge Gleeson's ruling broadens the scope of the law in this area.

"Nobody has said before that if you put an alien into the criminal process, his rights are any different than a citizen's," Mr. Winger said.

Plaintiffs' counsel contend that the men, though never charged with crimes, were in the early stage of a criminal process once they were detained.

Ernesto H. Molina Jr., senior litigation counsel for the Office of Immigration Litigation at the U.S. Department of Justice, acted as the lead attorney for the government.

Judge Gleeson is also presiding over another suit involving similar abuse claims, Elmaghraby v. Ashcroft , 04 CV 1409. That suit involves two plaintiffs, one of whom recently settled with the government for $300,000.

4

Family Deported After Boy's Arrest at School

Immigrant Rights Concerns Raised; Police Say Action Was Appropriate

Brady McCombs

A Catalina High Magnet School student and his family were deported after school officials found marijuana in his backpack and called Tucson police, who notified the Border Patrol after learning the family was here illegally.

The incident caused concern among immigrant rights advocates, but Tucson police officials say the officer acted appropriately in calling Border Patrol agents to the school.

On Thursday, police responded to Catalina High after school officials found a small amount of marijuana in the backpack of a ninth-grader who appeared to be under the influence, said Chyrl Hill Lander, Tucson Unified School District spokeswoman..

Police asked the boy's parents to come to the school, at East Pima Street and North Dodge Boulevard.

When the officer asked to see the drivers' licenses of the boy's parents, they said they had been living illegally in the United States for six years and that their 17-year-old son and his brother, a 12-year-old sixth-grader at Doolen Middle School, were also here illegally, said Roberto Villasenor, assistant Tucson police chief.

The officer called the Border Patrol, which sent agents to the school, said Richard DeWitt, Tucson Sector spokesman. They took the boy and his parents into custody and escorted the family from the school, Lander said.

From there, they went to Doolen Middle School, where the couple's other son was waiting in the principal's office when the officer and agents arrived, she said.

The mother and two boys were processed and dropped off at the border by the Border Patrol to return to Mexico in a procedure called voluntary return. The father was held for a formal removal -- formerly known as a deportation -- because he had been apprehended various times by the agency, DeWitt said. Their names were not released.

Police officials and the union said the officer handled the case correctly.

The boy had committed a crime, and the department's policy allows officers discretion to call the Border Patrol when they suspect someone they encounter is here illegally, Villasenor said.

"We can't lose track of the fact that an administrator came across a juvenile who was violating the law, in possession of marijuana," Villasenor said. "That is a crime in this country, whether you are here illegally or not."

But immigrants' rights groups say allowing immigration officials into schools could create distrust and fear in the immigrant community. TUSD officials said police should have waited to call immigration agents.

"We would have preferred that they called Border Patrol once they left the campus," said Lander, who was unaware of any other apprehensions made by the Border Patrol at TUSD schools. "There were rumors that it was a raid."

A long-standing police policy that was most recently reviewed in May prohibits officers from stopping anyone "merely on suspicion that the person is present in the United States illegally."

However, if after a stop for other reasons the officer believes the person is here illegally, the officer can ask immigration officials to come to the scene.

Officers have discretion on a case-by-case basis on whether to call immigration authorities, Villasenor said.

If Border Patrol agents can't respond or if it takes them too long to arrive, police officers can fill out a field interview form and release the person, according to the policy.

Reasonable suspicion is established if someone can't show a U.S. driver's license or immigration documentation, or sometimes an admission, which was the case with the boy's parents at Catalina High, Villasenor said. It cannot be based solely on skin color, he said.

"It's not reasonable to think that every Latino or Hispanic person is an illegal alien; that is not a reasonable suspicion," Villasenor said. "There has to be something much more than that."

Villasenor said the Police Department doesn't want crime victims or witnesses who are here illegally to fear coming forward because they might be deported.

The department isn't interested in its officers becoming immigration agents, either, he said.

"While we don't want to put a chilling effect on anyone calling us, we are also obligated to do our job," Villasenor said.

The Tucson Police Officers Association supports the policy, said union President Larry Lopez. It shouldn't matter where the crime is committed, he said.

"It doesn't matter if it's a school, a bank or grocery store; if they get called, they are going to respond," Lopez said.

The Border Patrol and Immigration and Customs Enforcement view schools more selectively.

"Typically, we won't enter the premises of churches or schools unless upon request of proper authorities or an emergency," said DeWitt, who called the school arrest a rarity.

ICE, which wasn't involved in Thursday's arrest but is responsible for enforcing immigration laws in the interior of the country, doesn't generally target churches and schools, said spokesman Vincent Picard. But that doesn't preclude them from making arrests at those locations if necessary, he said.

The incident at Catalina High could have wider implications, said an immigrant rights advocate.

"Now you have people who are afraid to call the police when they have been robbed because they are afraid the police will come and instead of investigating the crime will ask them about their immigration status," said Jennifer Allen, director of Tucson-based Border Action Network.

TUSD officials said they are dedicated to educating all children and don't worry about immigration status. "We hope it does not have a negative effect, and that all of our parents and guardians feel safe coming into our schools," Lander said.

On StarNet: Should Tucson police be helping to enforce immigration law? To vote in our poll, find this story online at azstarnet.com

"While we don't want to put a chilling effect on anyone calling us, we are also obligated to do our job." Roberto Villasenor, Tucson's assistant police chief

5

Immigration Agents Close by in Crackdown on Criminals

Some Say Operation Crossed Line of Public Safety, Personal Rights

Katie Fairbank

Gov. Rick Perry's office pitched Operation Wrangler to the public as a statewide crackdown on cross-border criminals -- gang members and smugglers of drugs and humans. Illegal immigrants were not targets, officials said. But immigration agents were not far away while police worked the operation. An immigration official said the agency set up "deportation and removal" sites and questioned immigrants on police officers' cellphones after some traffic stops. At least 137 people were returned to Mexico from North Texas during the weeklong operation. The hand-in-glove collaboration between local and federal agents won applause from advocates of stronger immigration enforcement, who called it a pragmatic way of dealing with a growing problem.

Some civil liberties groups, meanwhile, said they were frightened by the ways that the joint operation weakened the already blurry line between public safety and personal freedom. Mexican Consul Enrique Hubbard Urrea called it a form of racial profiling. The law requires probable cause before arrests are made, but Mr. Hubbard said he believes that some law enforcement officers acted as immigration agents during the operation and that people were pulled over because they were Hispanic.

"It doesn't seem to be clear here why they were stopped," Mr. Hubbard said. "There has to be a cause." Standard procedure Under state law, sworn officers are forbidden to ask about immigration status unless they've had specialized training.

"Unlawful presence" is a federal civil offense, although repeat offenders can ultimately face federal criminal violations. Local officers questioned about their participation in Operation Wrangler say they didn't pose such questions and were not out to catch illegal immigrants. But Carl Rusnok, a regional spokesman for U.S. Immigration and Customs Enforcement, known as ICE, said immigration agents were at times on site with police during traffic stops. Other times, officers who made the stops called agents and handed their cellphones to detainees. Police say some of the people were neither ticketed nor charged with any crime. "They [immigration officials] may ask to talk to people in the car and talk to them via cellphone," Mr. Rusnok said. "They then can ask them pointed questions over whether they are in the country legally or illegally." Mr. Rusnok said such cooperation is standard procedure and has been for years. "We routinely support other law enforcement," he said. Jose Alfredo Gonzalez, 18, a former resident of Grand Prairie, said he and three other construction workers were sent back to Mexico after they were stopped on Interstate 20 east of Dallas on Jan. 22. Mr. Gonzalez said an officer stopped the vehicle for speeding, which they deny doing. The officer spent several minutes on a cellphone, and then immigration agents showed up. "I would say the policeman called immigration," Mr. Gonzalez said by telephone from San Luis Potosi, Mexico. Law enforcement officials bristled at the suggestion that local officers acted the part of immigration agents during traffic stops, but they referred questions about the operation to the governor's office.

The governor's office has said only that the operation involved 90 sheriff's offices and 133 police departments, along with state troopers and other agencies, whose goal was to provide a law enforcement "surge" that would disrupt human smuggling and drug traffic. The state has refused to say which local departments participated or give any figures on the number of people ticketed or arrested. "We can't comment on any specific situation. This particular operation did not target illegal immigration," said Katherine Cesinger, a spokeswoman for Mr. Perry. "I can tell you that ICE is certainly integrated in Operation Wrangler. This targeted all crime. So if anyone was pulled over for any reason, if a law officer could not do a duty, they should call the appropriate authorities." The Dallas Police Department says it did not participate, but the Dallas County sheriff's office did, making 283 traffic stops that were related to the operation. Of those, 99 citations were written and nine people arrested, according to a department official who said one person was turned over to ICE after his arrest. Mr. Rusnok said ICE made 659 arrests and seized $88,000 during the operation. Of those immigrants arrested, at least 72 had criminal convictions, he said. Mr. Hubbard said his staff at the Mexican Consulate in Dallas interviewed people who were detained in the operation and heard story after story about groups of Hispanic workers stopped while traveling together in trucks. The workers told consular officials that police would ask for their identification, and an immigration agent would soon appear. Reyna Espinoza said her husband, Adelfo Neri Aguirre, was in a group of 11 immigrants from Mexico and Central America who were detained while riding in a van with a broken taillight in Denton County. According to Ms. Espinoza, an officer asked for immigration papers and then turned the group over to federal officials. Mr. Hubbard said his office is aware of at least 137 people in North Texas who were stopped under the same pattern and returned to Mexico as part of Operation Wrangler. A list of those people, compiled by the consulate, included three toddlers who were born in the U.S. Mr. Rusnok said the government typically sends U.S.-born children to Mexico with their parents if the parents make that request.

'Blurs the line' Collaboration between local police and federal immigration agents in this way is "creative in a very scary way," said Paul Heller, president of the Dallas chapter of the American Civil Liberties Union. "Certainly, it blurs the line dramatically," he said. "Obliterates it might be more accurate." A similar state effort along the border, Operation Linebacker, caused similar complaints last year. "What is new about Wrangler is it extends inland along trade corridors. Basically, our fear is that state funds will be used for state-sponsored racial profiling," said state Sen. Eliot Shapleigh, an El Paso Democrat. For police departments, it's a change in philosophy to get involved in immigration law. In the past, they tried to keep their distance for fear of losing hard-earned trust in the communities they protect. "Without the Hispanic community trusting the police, we would have a hard time doing what we do. We need victims and witnesses of crimes, regardless of status, to contact us," said Johanna Abad, spokeswoman for the Houston Police Department, which says it participated in Operation Wrangler. State law prevents police officers from arresting illegal immigrants unless they are charged with a criminal offense. And police departments interested in checking immigration status would have to send officers through special federal training.

"We're not authorized to check for citizenship. It's against the law for us to check. We're not trained in that, and we don't do that," said Michael Ortiz, a spokesman for the Dallas County Sheriff's Department.

Even so, there has been an evolution in practice. For instance, many Texas police departments decided during the past few years that it was OK to bring in immigration officials if an illegal immigrant is being held on a criminal charge. Dallas built an office for immigration agents at the Lew Sterrett Justice Center for that purpose. After an illegal immigrant was charged with killing a Houston police officer last fall, that department clarified that it was allowable for federal officials to check immigration status after an arrest.

Bob Dane, spokesman for the Federation for American Immigration Reform, said police are in a tough spot that would be unnecessary if existing federal immigration laws were better enforced. He is in favor of officers getting proper training in identification and detention techniques to avoid any problems. "The local enforcement that you see is really a reaction to inaction in Washington," Mr. Dane said.

Al Dia reporters Sergio Chapa and Isabel C. Morales contributed to this report.

6

Tortured Reasoning

The U.S. Department of Justice Attorneys Who Advised the White House on Military Prisoner Policy Bear Responsibility - Both Ethical and Moral - for the Abuse Scandals.

Stephen Gillers

Are the lawyers who advised the military that prisoners captured in Afghanistan were not protected by the laws of war morally responsible for the subsequent abuse? When this question is asked about conventional legal work, most lawyers answer no--a lawyer's job is to tell clients their legal options, with the client alone responsible for its choices. Whatever the validity of this view for ordinary work, however, it is wrong when the advice is from government lawyers, concerns the treatment of prisoners, is selective, and advocates a view likely to lead to violation of fundamental human rights guarantees.

In a January 9, 2002, memorandum to William Haynes II, general counsel of the U.S. Department of Defense, deputy assistant attorneys general John Yoo, a University of California law professor then on leave, and Robert Delahunty argued that neither the Third nor Fourth Geneva Conventions protected Al Qaeda and Taliban detainees captured in Afghanistan. Geneva III protects POWs from "physical or mental torture [or] any other form of coercion ... to secure ... information of any kind whatever." Geneva IV protects civilians "against all acts of violence or threats thereof" and protects women against "rape ... or any form of indecent assault." Also unavailable, the memo concludes, was "common Article 3" to the Conventions, which protects detainees even if the Conventions do not, and which forbids "violence to life and person ... cruel treatment and torture" and "outrages upon personal dignity, in particular humiliating and degrading treatment." The federal war crimes statute was irrelevant as well, the lawyers argued, because it defines "war crimes" to be a violation of the Geneva Conventions and Article 3. Nor did the "customary international laws of war" bind the president because it was not federal law. White House counsel Alberto Gonzales relied on this advice in his recommendations to the president, who adopted them.

The Yoo-Delahunty memo is at best incomplete. Although the first sentence of the 42-page memo says the authors were responding to a request for "our Office's views concerning the effect of international treaties and federal law on the treatment of" detainees from Afghanistan, it ignores duties imposed by the Convention against Torture and Other Cruel, Inhuman or Degrading Treatment or Punishment (which the United States ratified with reservations in 1994) and the federal torture statute, which creates criminal liability for U.S. nationals who commit torture abroad under color of law. Explicitly and by omission, then, the lawyers told the government it could treat detainees from Afghanistan as though they existed outside the rule of law. The government could offer legal protections voluntarily, but it need not, and the memo "expresses no view as to whether the President should" do so. Although the lawyers advised only on the treatment of Al Qaeda members and Taliban militia, some degree of misidentification was of course inevitable.

We are slowly learning the consequences of the advice. "We were pretty much told that they [Afghan prisoners] were nobodies, that they were just enemy combatants," one military police officer told The New York Times. "We called them hajis, and that psychology was really important." (Haji is a pejorative term for an Iraqi.) Human Rights Watch has reported arrests of Afghans and other nationals "with no apparent connection to ongoing hostilities" and has "documented numerous cases of mistreatment of detainees ... including extreme sleep deprivation, exposure to freezing temperatures ... severe beatings [and] being stripped ... and photographed while naked." Military doctors have called the death of two Bagram air base detainees homicides. Officers responsible for prisoner interrogation in Afghanistan and at Guantanamo Bay, Cuba, were later assigned to Abu Ghraib prison in Iraq. Eerily, descriptions of some of the Afghanistan abuses mirror what appeared in pictures from Iraq.

Legal ethics questions are often confused with questions of moral responsibility. The two are distant cousins, but here they converge. The ethical issue is simple. Failing to give a client an accurate, complete picture of the law is incompetence at best. As an adviser, a lawyer is not an advocate. Of course, a lawyer may urge particular conduct, but his preference must not skew the presentation of options. Human rights lawyers and others claim that the Yoo-Delahunty memo fails the test of accuracy and completeness. "It is not only wrong, it lays the groundwork for the commission of war crimes. It fails to recognize contrary U.S. military doctrine on the points it makes or to disclose credible sources that take different positions," says Scott Horton, president of the International League for Human Rights, and an adjunct teacher at Columbia Law School. Kenneth Roth, executive director of Human Rights Watch, faults the memo for failing to address the Convention against Torture. "When they say certain people are outside the Geneva Conventions and don't bother to mention parallel provisions of the Torture Convention, they invite wholesale abuse," he says. Colin Powell, secretary of State, wrote in a January 26, 2002, memorandum to Gonzales that denying applicability of the Geneva Conventions in Afghanistan "will reverse over a century of U.S. policy and practice ... and undermine the protections of the law of war for our troops, both in this specific conflict and in general." In an e-mail message, Yoo declined to respond to this criticism, citing "an ethical obligation to my former client not to discuss the nature of the legal advice given." Delahunty did not reply to an e-mail.

A lawyer's moral responsibility goes beyond ethical duties. Corporate wrongdoing, for example, has often led to questions about the responsibility of lawyers whose aggressive advice facilitated the misconduct. "Where were the lawyers?" the public, and even judges, have asked in the wake of these periodic scandals, including today. The answer, too often, is that the lawyers were enablers--giving advice that allowed the behavior that led to the frauds, the bankruptcies, and the massive financial harm. Critics argue that a gladiator role for lawyers may be tolerable in litigation, where it is balanced by an opposing gladiator and supervised by a judge, and where court records are presumptively public. But office advice is different. It is given in private and beyond adversarial challenge or judicial review, except in the event of litigation after the harm is done. Critics reject the idea that lawyers can give any advice a client wants to hear if they can manage to support it with nonfrivolous arguments. But many in the bar disagree. They say that respect for the autonomy of the client requires lawyers to identify even highly aggressive legal theories that will permit clients to pursue their goals, so long as the client knows the risks.

That debate will continue, but there should be no debate about the Yoo-Delahunty memo. For several reasons, its authors must accept moral responsibility for the abuse to which acceptance of their position has led. First, even though the client asked about “international treaties and federal laws” governing the treatment of the prisoners, the memo did not analyze the Convention against Torture and the federal torture statute. Second, as government lawyers, the authors had a heightened responsibility to the public interest and to be aware and warn of the harm to which their advice (exemption from the laws of war) might lead. Third, after arguing for these exemptions, the memo describes no legal restraint on the treatment of the prisoners. So far as a client reading the memo could know, prisoners taken in Afghanistan existed in a lawless world unless the president chose otherwise. Fourth, in its omissions and tone, the memo is a single-minded piece of advocacy, not a balanced analysis of the law. The advocacy includes Pollyannaish assurances that the advice poses no threat that captured U.S. soldiers might be subject to a reciprocal lawless fate. Although it might appear “counter-intuitive,” the authors write, the “President may still use his constitutional war-making authority to subject members of al Qaeda or the Taliban militia to the laws of war.”

These are failures of commission and omission. Perhaps, however, someone high in government explained that complete and balanced advice was not the client’s wish, that the client instead wanted arguments to support decisions already made. If this is what happened, then the lawyers might claim that they simply did their client’s bidding and, so long as their advice had some merit, they cannot be blamed for the consequences. But no. If the memo was meant to legitimate the client’s predetermined end, the lawyers are still to blame because they would have chosen to give the client the advice it wanted when the dangers of doing so--of consigning prisoners to a lawless state--were obvious. The recent death of Archibald Cox reminds us that lawyers are free to say no, just as Cox said no when Richard Nixon wanted him to curtail the Watergate investigation. But the lawyers here said yes. With that choice comes responsibility for the consequences.

Stephen Gillers is professor of legal ethics at New York University School of Law.

InfoMarks: Make Your Mark

What is an InfoMark?

It is a single-click return ticket to any page, any result, or any search from InfoTrac College Edition.

An InfoMark is a stable URL, linked to InfoTrac College Edition articles that you have selected. InfoMarks can be used like any other URL, but they're better because they're stable – they don't change. Using an InfoMark is like performing the search again whenever you follow the link, whether the result is a single article or a list of articles.

How Do InfoMarks Work?

If you can "copy and paste," you can use InfoMarks.

When you see the InfoMark icon on a result page, its URL can be copied and pasted into your electronic document – web page, word processing document, or email. Once InfoMarks are incorporated into a document, the results are persistent (the URLs will not change) and are dynamic.

Even though the saved search is used at different times by different users, an InfoMark always functions like a brand new search. Each time a saved search is executed, it accesses the latest updated information. That means subsequent InfoMark searches might yield additional or more up-to-date information than the original search with less time and effort.

Capabilities

InfoMarks are the perfect technology tool for creating:

- Virtual online readers
- Current awareness topic sites – links to periodical or newspaper sources
- Online/distance learning courses
- Bibliographies, reference lists
- Electronic journals and periodical directories
- Student assignments
- Hot topics

Advantages

- Select from over 15 million articles from more than 5,000 journals and periodicals
- Update article and search lists easily
- Articles are always full-text and include bibliographic information
- All articles can be viewed online, printed, or emailed
- Saves professors and students time
- Anyone with access to InfoTrac College Edition can use it
- No other online library database offers this functionality
- FREE!

How to Use InfoMarks

There are three ways to utilize InfoMarks – in HTML documents, Word documents, and Email.

HTML Document

1. Open a new document in your HTML editor (Netscape Composer or FrontPage Express).
2. Open a new browser window and conduct your search in InfoTrac College Edition.
3. Highlight the URL of the results page or article that you would like to InfoMark.
4. Right-click the URL and click Copy. Now switch back to your HTML document.
5. In your document, type in text that describes the InfoMarked item.
6. Highlight the text and click on Insert, then on Link in the upper bar menu.
7. Click in the link box, then press the "Ctrl" and "V" keys simultaneously and click OK. This will paste the URL in the box.
8. Save your document.

Word Document

1. Open a new Word document.
2. Open a new browser window and conduct your search in InfoTrac College Edition.
3. Check items you want to add to your Marked List.
4. Click on Mark List on the right menu bar.

5. Highlight the URL, right-click on it, and click Copy. Now switch back to your Word document.
6. In your document, type in text that describes the InfoMarked item.
7. Highlight the text. Go to the upper bar menu and click on Insert, then on Hyperlink.
8. Click in the hyperlink box, then press the "Ctrl" and "V" keys simultaneously and click OK. This will paste the URL in the box.
9. Save your document.

Email

1. Open a new email window.
2. Open a new browser window and conduct your search in InfoTrac College Edition.
3. Highlight the URL of the results page or article that you would like to InfoMark.
4. Right-click the URL and click Copy. Now switch back to your email window.
5. In the email window, press the "Ctrl" and "V" keys simultaneously. This will paste the URL into your email.
6. Send the email to the recipient. By clicking on the URL, he or she will be able to view the InfoMark.